Hiking Utah's County High Points

Alicia Baker

www.UtahCountyHighPoints.com
www.GirlonaHike.com

Photo Cover by Ian Boyer.

Visit the book website at
www.UtahCountyHighPoints.com

For more trail guides, visit the author's website at
www.GirlonaHike.com

County High Points

Rank	County	Peak	Elevation (ft)	Prominence (ft)	Page	Date Completed
26	Rich	Bridger Peak	9,255	855	6	
25	Davis & Morgan	Thurston Peak	9,706	2,690	9	
24	Weber	Willard Peak	9,763	3,243	12	
23	Box Elder	Bull Mountain	9,934	3,734	15	
22	Cache	Naomi Peak	9,979	3,159	18	
21	Kane	Kane County High Point	10,080	0	20	
20	Millard	Mine Camp Peak	10,222	3,001	23	
19	Washington	Signal Peak	10,365	4,485	26	
18	Carbon	Monument Peak	10,452	1,617	29	
17	Emery	East Benchmark	10,743	1,543	31	
16	Wasatch	Murdock Mountain-West Slope	10,840	0	34	
15	Tooele	Deseret Peak	11,031	5,812	36	
14	Sanpete	South Tent Mountain	11,285	3,365	39	
13	Iron	Brian Head	11,307	3,747	42	

Rank	County	Peak	Elevation (ft)	Prominence (ft)	Page	Date Completed
12	Wayne	Bluebell Knoll	11,320	2,900	44	
11	Salt Lake	American Fork Twin Peaks	11,489	3,649	47	
10	Garfield	Mount Ellen	11,522	5,842	50	
9	Sevier	Fish Lake Hightop	11,633	4,153	53	
8	Utah	Mount Nebo	11,928	5,488	56	
7	Juab	Ibapah Peak	12,087	5,247	59	
6	Beaver & Piute	Delano Peak	12,169	4,689	62	
5	Daggett & Uintah	Eccentric Benchmark	12,276	716	65	
4	Grand	Mount Waas	12,331	1,793	68	
3	San Juan	Mount Peale	12,721	6,161	71	
2	Summit	Gilbert Peak	12,442	1,554	74	
1	Duchesne	King's Peak	13,528	6,348 ft	78	

Bonus Peaks

Peak	Elevation (ft)	Effort	Page	Date Completed
Clayton Peak	10,721	Easy	82	
Mt.Ogden	9,579	Easy	85	
Frary Peak	6,578	Easy	88	
Bald Mountain	11,942	Easy	91	
Reids Peak	11,708	Medium	95	
Mt.Superior	11,040	Medium	98	
Lewis Peak	8,031	Medium	101	
Grandeur Peak	8,299	Medium	104	
Spanish Fork Peak	10,192	Medium	107	
Santaquin Peak	10,685	Medium	110	
Lookout Peak	8,954	Medium	113	
Mill Canyon Peak	10,349	Medium	116	
Fool Creek Peak	9,712	Medium	119	

Peak	Elevation (ft)	Effort	Page	Date Completed
Mt.Elliott	7,142	Medium	122	
Lone Peak	11,251	Hard	126	
Grandview Peak	9,410	Hard	130	
Provo Peak	11,068	Hard	133	
Mt.Timpanogos	11,752	Hard	136	
Wellsville Cone	9,356	Hard	140	
Box Elder Peak	11,101	Hard	143	

Introduction

I moved to Utah in 2013 and had no idea that peak-bagging would become a "thing" for me. I've always loved to hike and would enjoy having a destination, usually a lake or waterfall, but those can be somewhat scarce in Utah. I had made friends with people who liked to do this thing called peak-bagging — hiking with the goal to reach the top of a mountain. I didn't really think much of it; I was just happy to get outside, be with friends, and reach a new type of destination — the summit. I didn't know it back then that I had started on this journey to hiking high points, some of those which were included in County high points. This was back in 2014.

Over the years, I had slowly done several peaks that I didn't even know were included in this list of high points. At one point, one of my friends said, "Hey, you've only got two peaks left to finish the Utah Ultra Prominence Peaks!" I replied, "Well, what is that and what are they?" He described it to me, and I was on a mission to finish those last two peaks that same year.

After that list was complete, I started to look at all the peaks I had done and then realized I was halfway done with the county high points. I knew this was another list I just had to finish. Oh, and it helped that I had made another friend who was working on the same list, so of course, I wanted to finish it before him! I had my priorities in order and in one year, I finished the other half. The total time for me to complete all the County High Points was five years! It takes most people a few years to complete them all, but it's not unheard of to do it in one year.

Why County High Points?

One of the best things about having a goal to complete all County High Points is that it took me to parts of Utah I never thought I'd explore. It got me to step out of my comfort zone, explore new mountain ranges and helped me learn to enjoy the "not so pretty parts" of Utah. Exploring all these summits generally gets you away from people, except extremely popular summits such as Mt.Timpanogos or Mt.Nebo, for example. It gets you away from crowds, allows you to explore something completely new, you get a free full-body workout without having to go to a gym, you can choose to spend time alone or with friends, and the fresh air feeds the soul.

Gear Recommendations

See my hiking gear checklist on page 147.

Mountain Safety

Hiking in Utah can be dangerous. All readers must assume responsibility for their own actions and safety. This book will not replace decision-making skills and/or experience, which help reduce risk exposure. Learn as much as possible about hiking and backpacking first before venturing into the mountains. Here are just a few tips about mountain safety.

Access

The first thing to consider when planning a summit hike is how to get to the trailhead. In some cases, you will need 4x4 drive to reach the trail, unless you want to mountain bike sections or turn your hike into a longer one.

Clothing

The most important item of clothing is your footwear. Your shoes must be comfortable and durable. Many of these peaks are rocky and you will need good tread to keep from slipping too easily. My personal preference of a hiking/backpacking shoe are trail runners; however, a lot of my friends prefer heavier boots. It's really up to you - just make sure you can comfortably hike up to 10 miles or more a day in them without them tearing or giving you blisters. That leads to good socks. Make sure you are not wearing just cotton socks - get a mixture of merino wool, lycra, and/or spandex. A favorite brand of mine is Darn Tough.

As for the clothes on your back, also make sure these are not fully cotton. A mixture of materials is best, especially for people who sweat heavily. As your sweat and body temperature cools, you want your clothes to dry, not hang on to that wetness, making you cold. Dress in layers and consider carrying a pair of lightweight pants in case you find yourself in thick bushwhacking.

Water

Always carry a small water filter on your hikes (if a water source is available). You never know if you will run out of water (I have) and having a tiny water filter was key for me to continue hiking. Try to filter water from a moving source such as a creek and avoid stagnant water sources (if possible).

Maps

Make sure you know how to use and read a map and GPS. Carry extra batteries or a USB charging stick to access maps on your phone. Learn how to read topographic maps. If you need assistance on how to do this, YouTube is a great resource, and you can also check out your local outdoor sporting store for classes.

Weather

Be prepared for any kind of weather. Utah is well known for extreme weather changes in a matter of minutes. Be prepared with layers of clothing, the right types of jacket (wind vs rain vs down), and learn the signs and symptoms of hypothermia, frostbite, and dehydration. Always carry sunblock, a hat, and light gloves. If caught in a rainstorm, get off the ridge immediately, stay away from tall solitary trees, stay away from water, and keep out of shallow caves or overhangs. The best place to be is in a group of trees around the same height.

Leave No Trace

Stay on the trail

Shortcutting causes erosion and it doesn't save time on steep ascents plus increases the chance of injury.

Avoid Building Fires

Prohibited in many backcountry areas, they're extremely risky amid dry areas for fires, especially in the desert.

Pack everything out

Never leave trash behind, even if it isn't yours. This includes toilet paper, nut shells, fruit peels, etc. Keep a small bag handy, so picking up trash is easy and won't get your gear stinky.

Poop without impact

Choose a site to poop at least 70 yards away from trails and water sources. Dig a small hole about 4-8 inches deep. Afterwards, throw a handful of dirt into the hole to camouflage the site. Pack out toilet paper in a plastic ziplock bag. Carry a small-sized hand sanitizer bottle with you.

Other Leave No Trace Examples:

- Camp on previously used sites
- Leave wildflowers alone, do not pick them
- Respect the reverie of other hikers
- Respect wildlife - do not approach or follow them
- Hike in small groups when possible
- Do not erect new cairns

Dogs

This book's key aspect is focusing on how dog-friendly each trail is — most of my hikes are accompanied by my Golden Labrador, Charlie. I take him hiking whenever I can and when allowed, as he fully enjoys nature just as much as I do. For him to explore and experience what I like to do has created a special experience for us both. Always carry a leash and easily accessible in-case you come across wildlife or people who may be afraid of dogs. Be sure to carry plenty of water for your dog (or have them carry it in their own backpack), a first aid kit, and dog booties (if they tear a pad). Ensure your dog is trained to physically hike longer distances - start out hiking 2 or 3 miles, then gradually work up to 10 miles in a day. Just like humans need to train for long hikes, so do dogs. Don't risk them getting an injury in the middle of nowhere without cell service.

While there are plenty of resources for making the trek to each high point, I've compiled my experiences into one guidebook that I hope will assist you in your adventures.

I've included a trails checklist, detailed trail guides with a trail map for each hike, as well as a gear checklist at the end of the book. Take a screenshot of each peak and the checklist, then let's start hiking!

- Alicia Baker

Bridger Peak, Rich County

Stats

Distance: 1.3 miles to summit (half is off-trail)

Elevation gain: 918 ft

Time: 1 hour

Dog friendly? Yes, off-leash

Kid friendly? No, due to steepness and off-trail hiking

Fees/Permits? None

Best Season: Summer & Fall

Comment

Bridger Peak (9,225 Ft) is the Rich County High Point and the lowest in elevation of all Utah County High Points (CoHPs)! This is one of the most uneventful CoHPs, but alas, it is a must-do as a peak bagger! The trail is dog friendly with plenty of shade but no water.

Getting There

From Logan, UT, drive up Logan Canyon for 30 miles, then turn left at the signed "Swan Flat" road (FR041). The Swan Flat Road is 2.5 miles past the Beaver Creek Lodge. Reset your odometer and drive 3.4 miles along the dirt road. The trail starts on the right side of the road, marked by a worn-down fence and brown post. I wouldn't take a small car up this road, but an SUV or larger will be fine.

The Route

Start by following the trail by the boulder. You can also see a brown post from here. Drop down to the bottom of the small gully, then back up again. It gets really steep for the next 1/2 mile. Eventually, the views open up and you'll now be hiking south. At 0.7 miles, the trail opens up and you'll see the rock band on your left. From here, leave the trail and pick what looks like a good route to you to get to the top of the rock band. For the next 1/4 mile looks like a hike off-trail through the forest. Again, pick a route that looks good, aiming for the next small ridge on your GPS. When you reach the ridge you should now be able to see Bear Lake to the East! Continue following the ridge left (north). Keep going...the hiking along the ridge is really easy. There almost seemed to be a faint path left by all the previous peak baggers working on the CoHPs. There is an old, dead juniper tree near the summit. Even though you only hike off-trail for 0.6 miles, I highly recommended carrying a GPS or using Gaia GPS (what I've used for years) on your phone. On the way back, everything looked the same, so I had to keep looking at it to get me back to where I initially left the trail.

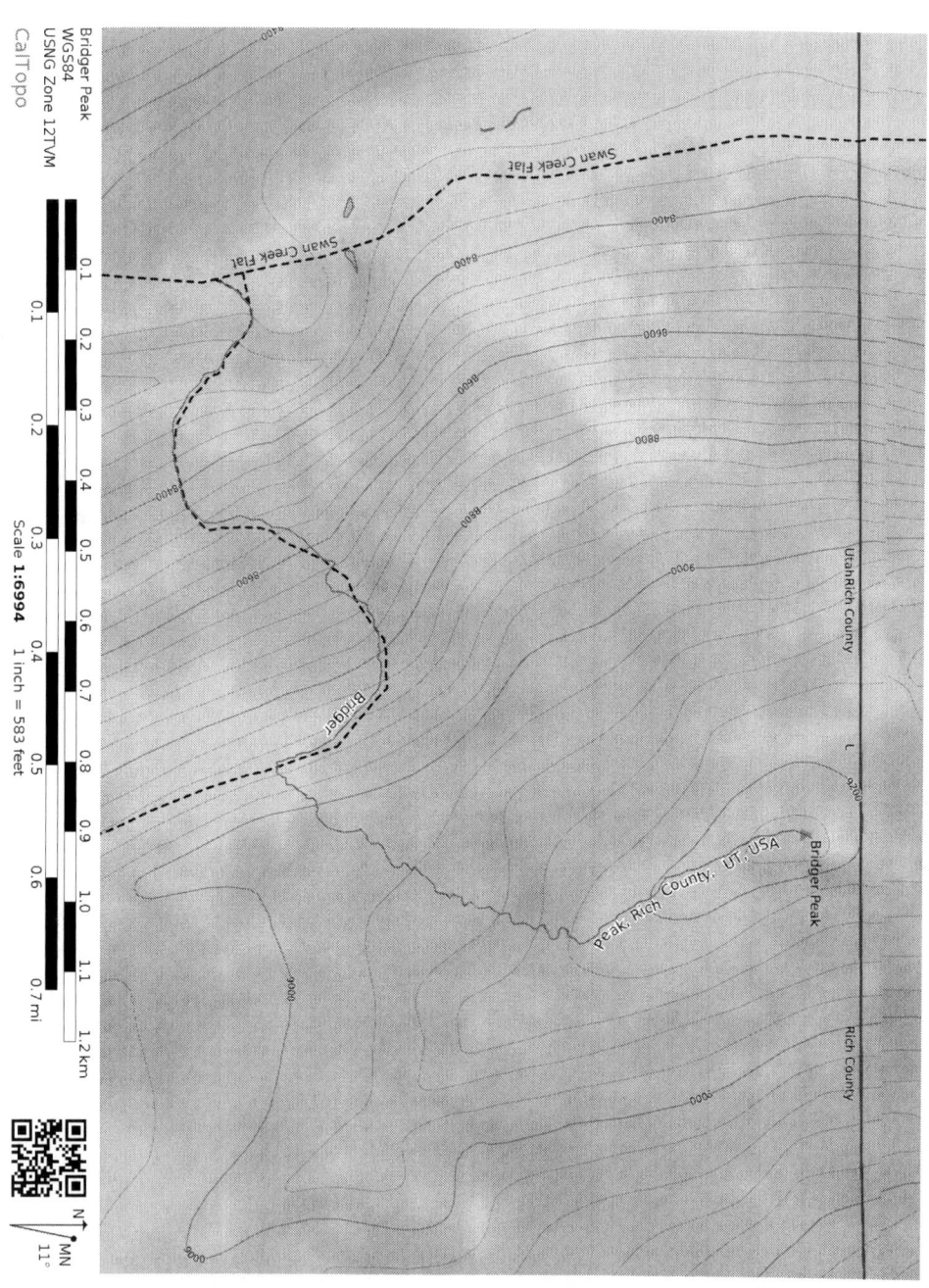

Thurston Peak, Morgan & Davis County

Stats

Distance: 8.4 miles RT

Elevation gain: 1,775 ft

Time: 4-6 hours

Dog friendly? Yes, off-leash

Kid friendly? Yes, but maybe not for the whole distance

Fees/Permits? None

Best Season: Summer & Fall

Comment

Thurston Peak (9,706 Ft) straddles the Davis-Morgan County line, making it the tallest peak for both counties. Many people think that Francis Peak, with the big white golf ball domes on the summit, is the highest peak along the ridge, but Thurston Peak claims the high point. This is a relatively easy peak for Peak Baggers to the summit, since it only gains 1,700 ft over 4.2 miles. The high alpine setting has expansive views all around - Antelope Island to the West, Mt. Ogden to the North, and an overview of Morgan, UT to the East.

Getting There

From SLC, head north on I-15 and take exit 395. Turn Right on Park Lane, then turn right again on Main St. Turn left onto 600 north, and turn left again onto 100 north. Drive 8 miles up Farmington Canyon. This quickly turns into a narrow dirt road, and a truck or jeep is ideal for driving this. A small car might make it, but after a recent storm or if a lot of ATVs use this road, it may be too rough. Once you reach two gates, turn left. And continue another 4.5 miles until you reach the large white radar/golf ball. Park here and begin hiking. There are no restrooms.

The Route

Start out by just walking along the old jeep road for about 1.75 miles. Stay left for FR206. Once the road ends, the narrow trail continues along the ridge. Rather than hiking over each unnamed peak, the trail dips along the slope to an elevation as low as 9,000 ft. The trail favors staying on the West side of the Ridge (the Davis County side), but a few times will stay on the East. The West side of the trail is dotted with sagebrush and grasslands - the Eastside is mostly pine trees. At exactly 4.0 miles, keep your eye out for a large cairn and trail split on another saddle. You'll leave the main trail and follow the cairns up a poorly defined trail along the ridge for the last 0.2 miles. This last section is pretty steep, but keep an eye out for cairns to help guide you. Pink and black, marbled granite dots this ridgeline and slope, which will help you to know you are in the right area to start ascending. You've reached the peak when you find the plaque and summit register.

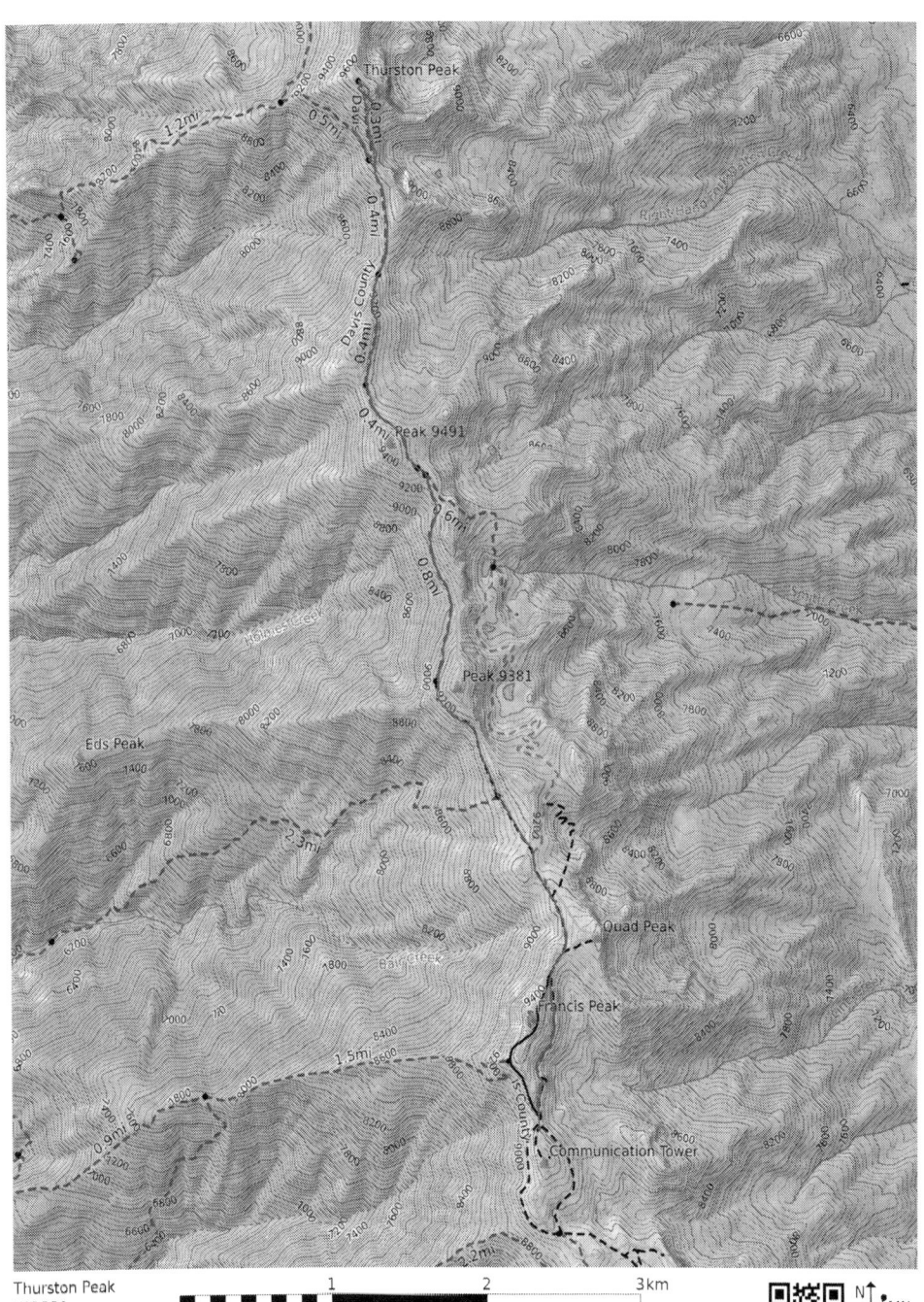

Thurston Peak
WGS84
USNG Zone 12TVL
CalTopo

Scale **1:30953**   1 inch = 2579 feet

Willard Peak, Weber County

Stats

Distance: 7.6 miles RT

Elevation gain: 1,500 ft

Time: 3-5 hours

Dog friendly? Yes, off-leash

Kid friendly? Yes (except for Willard Peak)

Fees/Permits? None

Best Season: Summer or Fall

Comment

Willard Peak (9,763 Ft) and Ben Lomond Peak (9,712 Ft) are the two high points dominating the Northern end of the Wasatch Mountains, above Ogden, Utah. Willard Peak is the high point for Weber County, though it sees less than half the number of hikers than the popular Ben Lomond Peak. Both are worthy summits, and to avoid having to come back on separate days to hike each one, do both in one trip.

There are several access points for starting your hike to each summit. The easiest way is via Willard Basin, which is only available to drive up from July 1 through October 31st (when the gates are open). Driving this narrow, winding, dirt road does require a 4X4 car such as a truck or jeep. Small, compact cars will not make it.

Both peaks are fairly easy, especially if you have some peak bagging experience. If you are a beginner hiker, you may find it more difficult. The trail starts from Willard Basin Campground and passes by a high alpine lake before reaching the ridge. The hike up to Willard Peak follows a very lightly tracked trail marked by cairns while hiking over to Ben Lomond is easier along a heavily trafficked trail due to popularity. The entire hike will offer amazing views of Willard Bay and the Great Salt Lake to the West, as well as the valleys to the East. On a clear day, you can see Mt. Ogden to the South as well.

Getting There

From SLC, head north on I-15 and take exit 362. Drive 5.1 miles along HWY 91, and take the exit for S 100 in Mantua, UT. Turn right on Main St, which then turns into Willard Peak Road. Follow this road, which turns into a dirt road. Once you are on the dirt road, it will take you an hour to reach the trailhead, even though it's only 8 miles away. Total drive time from SLC is about 2 hours. 4x4 is needed.

The Route

The trailhead is not marked off the dirt road, but it starts at the Willard Basin Campground. It is marked by a brown forest service pole and three large boulders. After you walk up about 100 yards, you should see the official trailhead sign. Reach the alpine lake, then the trail continues to the left and wind it's way up to the ridge. One switchback  will take you to the ridge. Once at the ridge, look for the very light trail that heads directly up the ridge leading to Willard Peak. You'll see a trail that goes left, but in a more downward direction - don't take that. As long as you stay on the ridge, you'll reach the peak. Keep an eye out for cairns. After hanging out at the summit, hike back down the same way you came up (the North ridge) instead of going down the South ridge. Back on the main trail, you will be hiking below Willard Peak, heading in a Southerly direction. The next 2 miles are the easiest, as you hike along a well-maintained trail to Ben Lomond Peak.

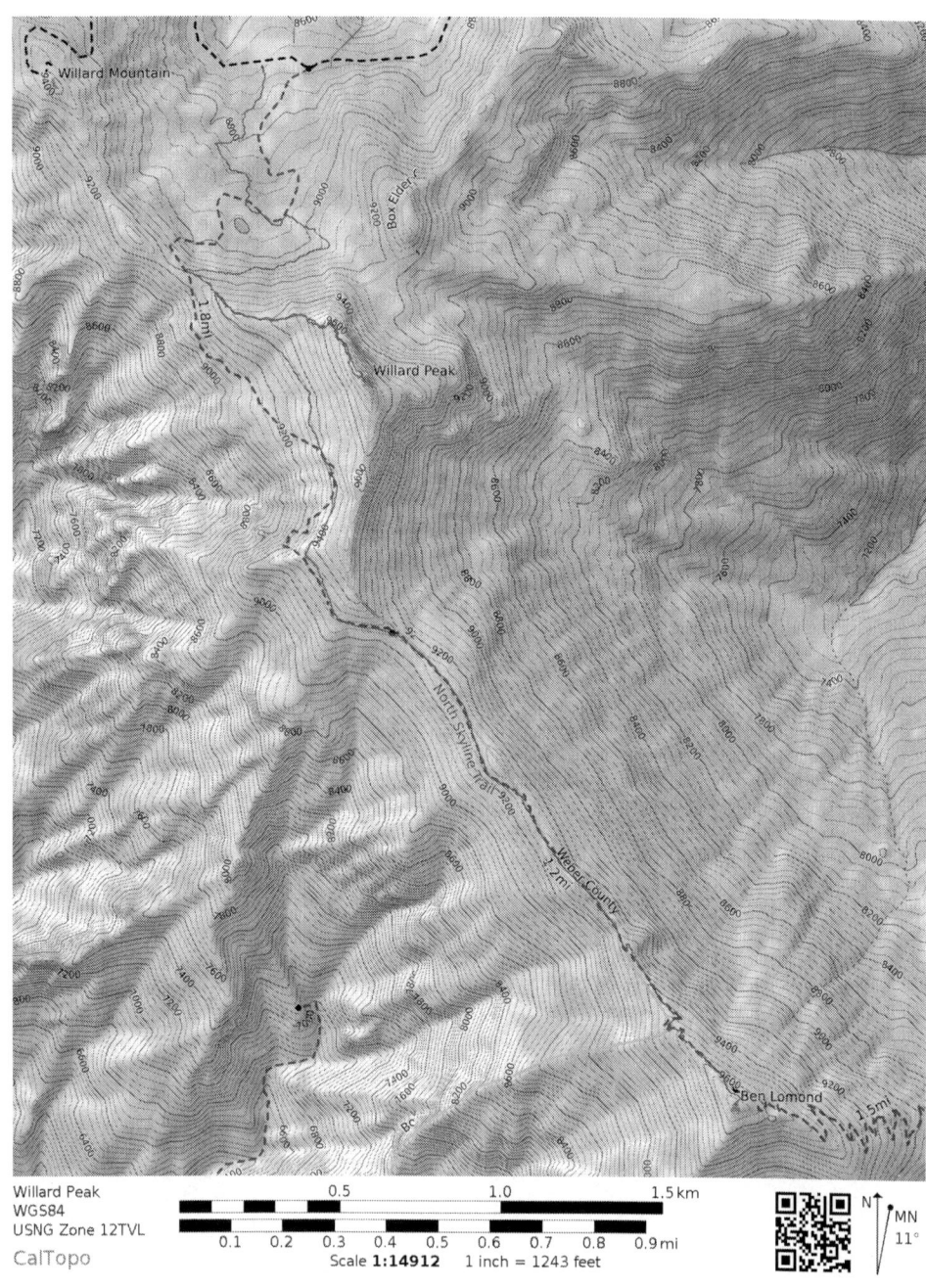

Willard Peak
WGS84
USNG Zone 12TVL
CalTopo

Scale **1:14912**   1 inch = 1243 feet

Bull Mountain, Box Elder County

Stats

    Distance: 11 miles RT

    Elevation gain: 3,587 ft

    Time: 5-7 hours

    Dog friendly? Yes, off-leash

    Kid friendly? No

    Fees/Permits? None

    Best Season: Summer & Fall

Comment

Bull Mountain (9,938 Ft) is the Box Elder County High Point and the highest peak in the Raft River Mountain Range. This range is a mix of desert-like terrain on the lower half and high alpine terrain on the upper half. This unique mix of land makes for a beautiful hike but is typically only accessible in summer and fall.

There are three ways to reach Bull Mountain:

1) Drive up the 4x4 dirt road - high clearance vehicle needed.

2) Lake Fork Trail - this trail fades out near the cirque and you will be left to do some heavy bushwhacking and Class 3-4 scrambling to reach the ridge.

3) Bull Flat Trail - this is the route I took. It stays more along the ridge, but there is one 3/4 mile long section with no trail. Otherwise, the trail is very easy to follow.

Camping is free and available right at the trailhead at the Clear Creek Campground. The trail is only half shaded and there is only one water source along the trail at the natural spring, just over halfway to the summit. This is a great trail for dogs, except we did see many foxtails along the way up.

Getting There

From SLC, drive north on I-15 and take exit 5 for Snowville, UT. Head west on UT-30, then veer right for UT-42. As your drive into Idaho, this road is now ID-81. Turn left on E. Naf Rd and drive 3.2 miles. Turn Left on S. Clear Creek Road (you'll now see brown signs) and drive for 2 miles, then right on Clear Creek

Road again. Continue following this as the road ends at the Clear Creek Campground.

The Route

The trail begins in the campground, just before the end of the road on the Southside (right) marked by a brown post "001". You'll quickly cut through a gate. At 0.8 miles, turn right for Bull Flat Trail. Going left will take you up the Lake Fork trail, which ends near the cirque. Cross a small creek, then start working uphill. You'll hike through desert-like terrain and a few  small switchbacks. It's consistently steep. There's a few sections that are a little overgrown but not bad. At 2.6 miles, you'll pass a large white rock. It looks to be a mix of sandstone/quartzite. After another two switchbacks and heading south along the ridge again, you'll reach the private property fence. There is no trail from here to the spring/pond — be prepared to hike through the sage field straight across. Make sure you have a GPS handy so you know where to aim towards the spring/pond. After you reach the spring/pond area, there is a spring just above the pond in a horse trough. If you wanted to backpack, this area would be the most ideal. It's the only water spot, and there are plenty of flat campsites to choose from. After hiking for another mile or so, the trail dies out again - just stay along the ridge. When you leave the tree line, start to aim for the actual summit, which actually isn't above the cirque at all but a little further out on top of Bull Flat. You'll pass through the private property gate again. The summit itself isn't much to look at. Return the way you came.

A word on the private property - I actually met the landowners on the summit and said, "I figured I'm just hiking through and will clean up trash, so it should be ok?" They responded, "Of course! We want hikers to come through here and be able to explore as long as they keep it clean." So they bought the land in early 2019 and want to spread the word that it is fully ok to hike through there (just pick up trash!).

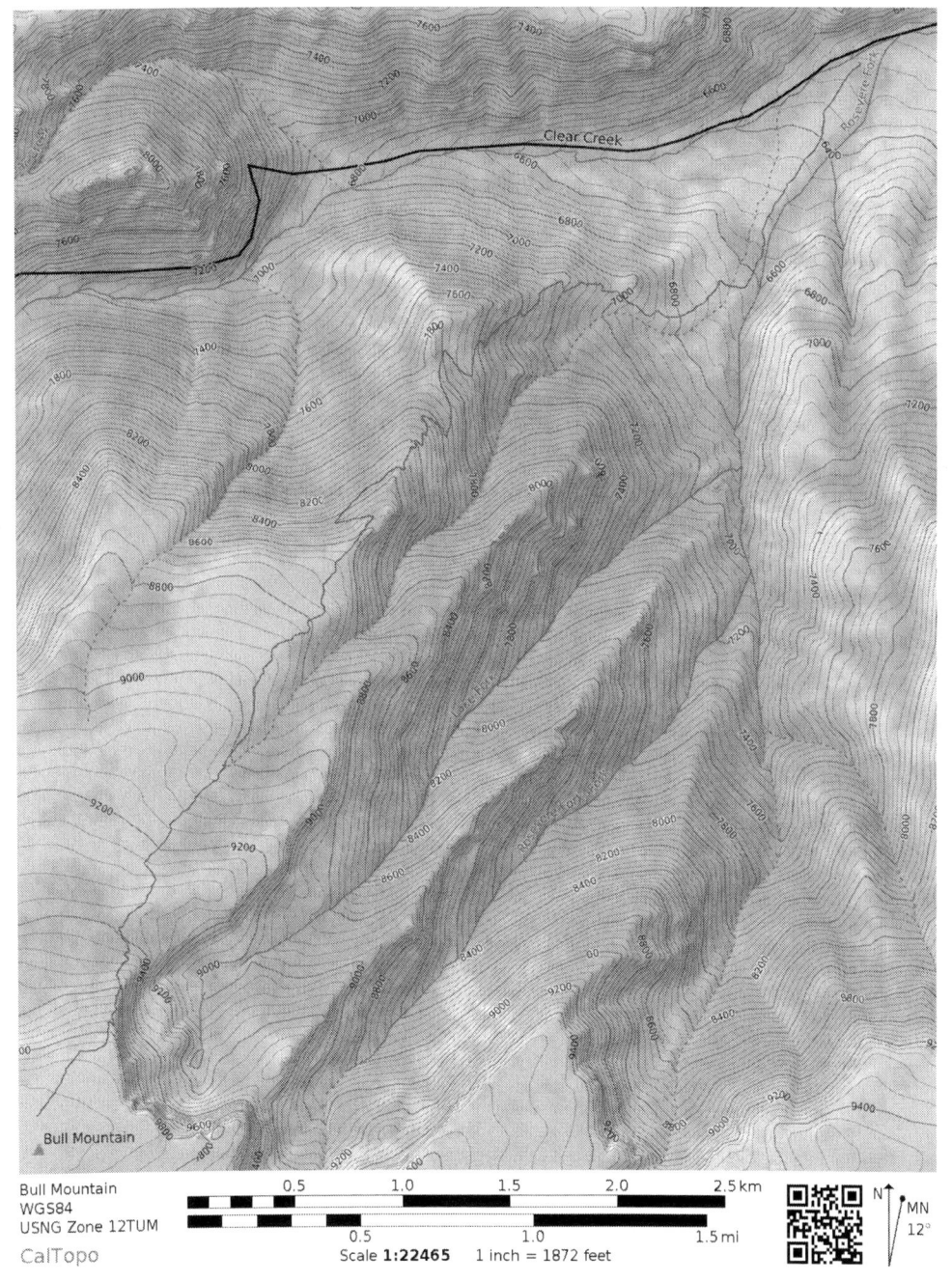

Clear Creek

Bull Mountain

Bull Mountain
WGS84
USNG Zone 12TUM

CalTopo

Scale **1:22465**   1 inch = 1872 feet

0.5   1.0   1.5   2.0   2.5 km

0.5   1.0   1.5 mi

N   MN 12°

Naomi Peak, Cache County

Stats

Distance: 6.6 miles RT

Elevation gain: 1,900 ft

Time: 3-6 hours

Dog friendly? Yes, off-leash

Kid friendly? No

Fees/Permits? $6/day parking fee. No Permit.

Best Season: Summer or Fall

Comment

Naomi Peak (9,983 Ft) is the highest point in the Bear River Mountains in Northern Utah. Most people make the summit from the trail starting at Tony Grove Lake, but you can also access the peak from Dry Canyon, which is on the West side of the mountain range. Starting from Tony Grove is on the East side of the mountains, travels through many wildflowers in early summer, a rock amphitheater, several meadows, and offers breathtaking views of Cache Valley and the surrounding peaks.

Getting There

From SLC, head north on I-15 and take exit 362. Stay on HWY 89 for 27 miles until you reach Logan, UT. Turn right onto 400 N, and drive another 22 miles. Look for the brown Tony Grove Lake sign. Drive another 7 miles to the large parking lot. The trail starts at the West end of the parking lot. There is one restroom in the parking lot.

The Route

The TH starts on the western side of the parking lot. Turn right for Naomi Peak. When you reach the 2nd trail split, turn left after 15 minutes of hiking, pass by the "rock amphitheater" on the left. At the 3rd trail, split, stay straight. Work your way up some small switchbacks, and eventually, you'll reach a small pass. Continue following the trail to the summit.

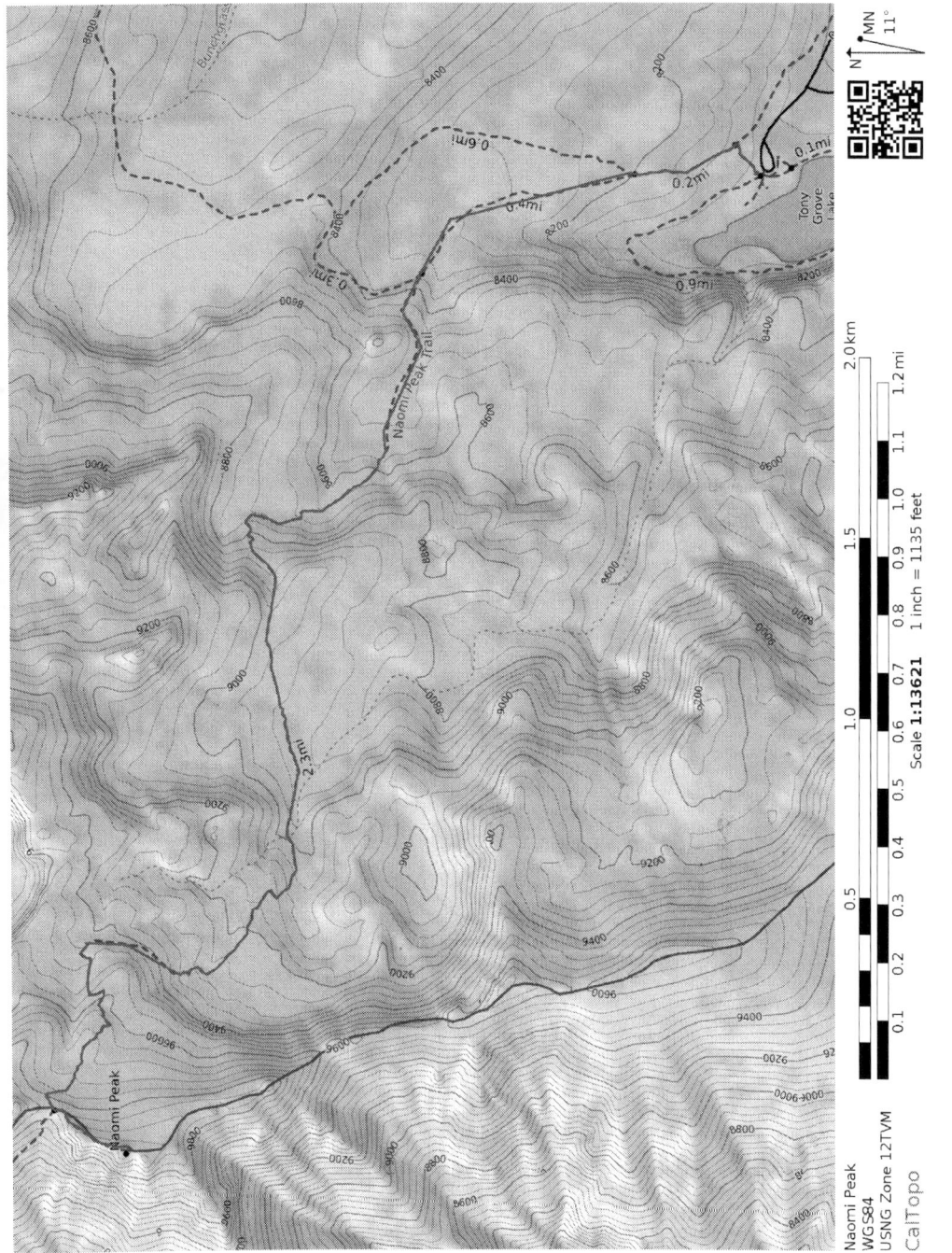

Naomi Peak
WGS84
USNG Zone 12TVM
CalTopo

Scale 1:13621

1 inch = 1135 feet

Kane County High Point, Kane County

Stats

Distance: 0.4 miles RT

(depending on how far your car can make it)

Elevation gain: flat

Time: 5-15 min RT

Dog friendly? Yes, off-leash

Kid friendly? Yes

Fees/Permits? None

Best Season: Summer or Fall

Comment

The Kane County High Point (10,080 Ft) is located on a small ridge rather than on an actual peak. The highest actual peak, Andy Nelson Peak (10,027 Ft) is nearby, so it is worth doing both on the same day. In one day, we actually did the Kane CoHP, Andy Nelson Peak, hiked Cascade Falls, drove through the lava fields, and then drove to the Iron County HP (Brian Head Peak).

Both peaks are very easy with only 4 miles RT for Andy Nelson Peak and a 10 minute RT hike for the Kane CoHP.

Camping near the THs is very easy, as Navajo Lake has three campgrounds available for $17/night. I highly recommend making a reservation ahead of time; however, walk-in sites are available first come, first serve as well.

Getting There

From Navajo Lake Lodge, drive back out to HWY 14 and turn left. Drive 3.1 miles and turn left on FR055. Drive 1.5 miles, then turn left on FR1642. If you are driving a small car, you'll want to park here and either hop in a friend's 4x4 car or start hiking from here. If you have a higher clearance car, continue straight for another mile or so, as far as your car can make it. We parked 5 minutes from the actual summit since the road got really rutted out and narrow.

The Route

Just past the 4-way intersection, the road started to get really narrow from trees, so we pulled over to park where we could. We started to hike from there. Follow the road to where it meets the ridge, then turn right, staying along the ridge/cliff. Hike through the trees, off-trail, to find the summit. We found the high point within 10 minutes of hiking. A small cairn and summit register mark it.

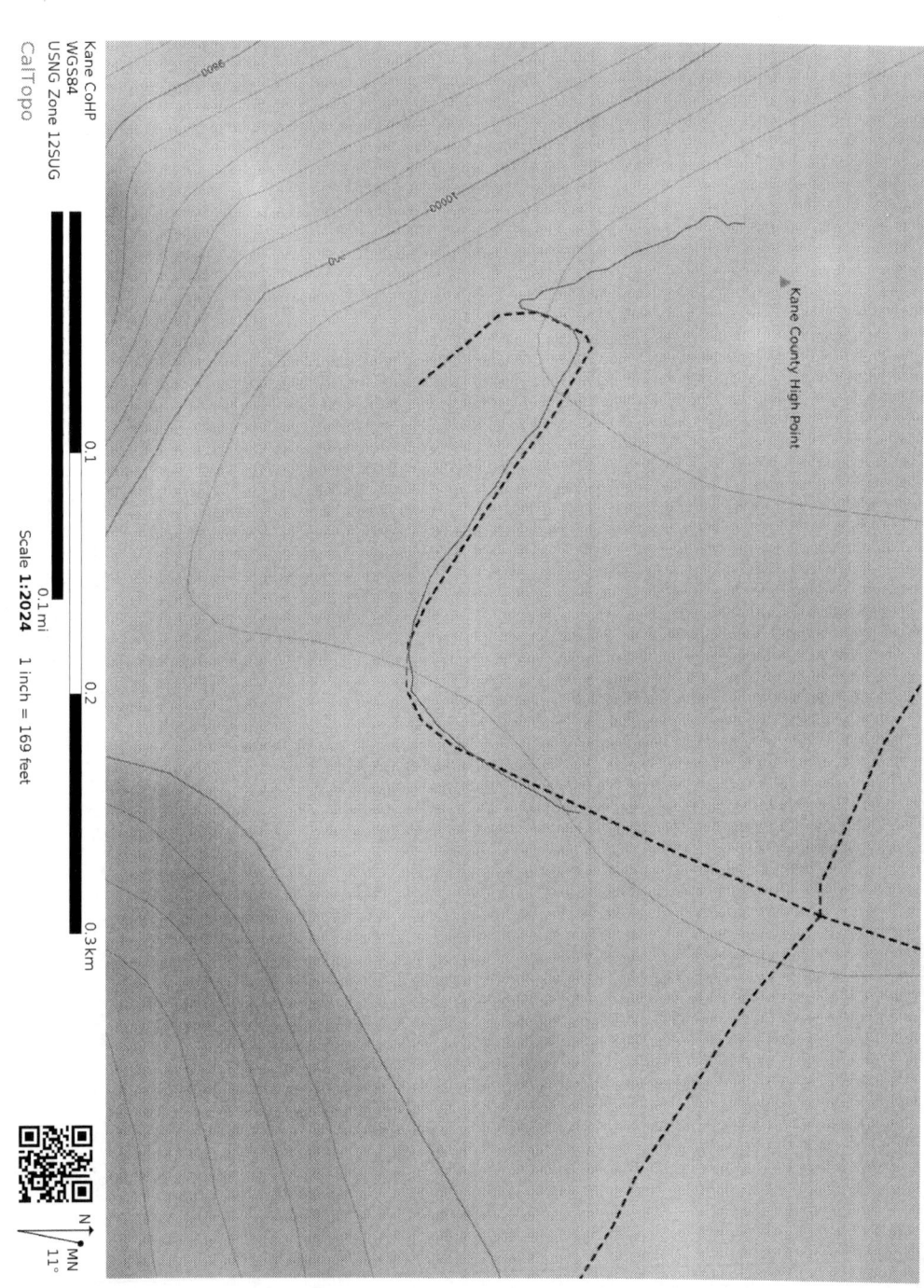

Kane CoHP
WGS84
USNG Zone 12SUG

CalTopo

Scale **1:2024** 1 inch = 169 feet

Kane County High Point

Mine Camp Peak, Millard County

Stats

Distance: 1 mile RT

Elevation gain: 375 ft

Time: 1 hour

Dog friendly? Yes, off-leash

Kid friendly? Yes, ages 6+

Fees/Permits? None

Best Season: Summer or Fall

Comment

Mine Camp Peak (10, 222ft) is the Millard County High Point and one of the easiest to summit out of all the CoHPs at only 1 mile round trip. The drive will take much longer than the actual hike, so be prepared to spend close to half a day at least to summit this peak and make the drive in and out. Mine Camp Peak should be combined with other peaks in the area since it's so short. In one weekend, we knocked out Brian Head Peak (Iron County High Point), Andy Nelson Peak & the Kane County High Point, Cascade Falls, and South Tent Mountain (Sanpete County High Point). Camping is available right at the trailhead, but only 2-3 tents can fit and one car can park there.

Getting There

From Richfield, head west on W 300 N. You'll pass under the I-70, then pass a large tan water tank. At 1.3 miles, pass the winter gate. At 8 miles, turn right for Chalk Creek Road. At 16 miles, left on Sand Creek Road. Total mileage along FR96 is only 18 miles but it will take you about 45 min to 1 hour to drive. A small car will have some trouble on this road, so an SUV or large is needed.

The easiest drive is to come up from Richfield, Utah. You can come up from Fillmore, Utah, but only if you have an ATV. The road on that side of the mountain is extremely bumpy, rutted out, and narrow. We talked to a family in an ATV coming up from that side, as we were debating to go down that way, and they highly suggested not to.

The Route

The official peak sign is *not* where the trail starts. The actual faint trail starts on the Northside of the cattle guard, up about 20 feet. Start by dropping down the faint trail on the Northside of the cattle guard. The trail drops down about 100 Ft to the saddle — pass a sinkhole. From the saddle, continue up the ridge to the peak. Stay on the far right of the ridge, or else you'll be trapped into bushwhacking. You should see a faint trail the whole way. Eventually, the trees fade away, and you'll be hiking across a more level field. Then just aim for the summit! It took us 18 minutes to reach Mine Camp Peak! There is a summit register.

@GirlonaHike.com

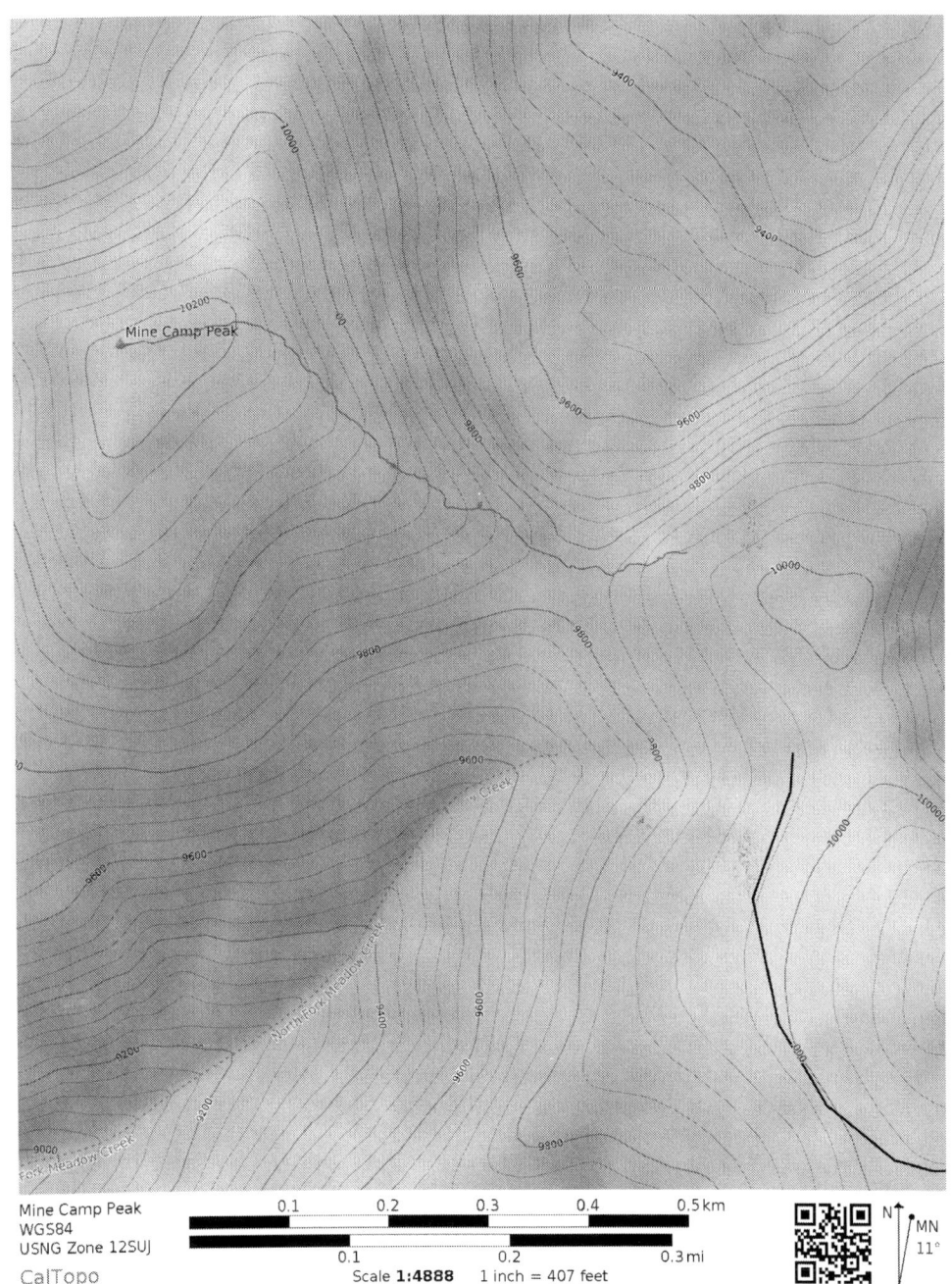

Mine Camp Peak
WGS84
USNG Zone 12SUJ

CalTopo

0.1   0.2   0.3   0.4   0.5 km

0.1   0.2   0.3 mi
Scale **1:4888**   1 inch = 407 feet

N
MN
11°

Signal Peak, Washington County

Stats

    Distance: 10 miles RT

    Elevation gain: 4,000 ft

    Time: 7-9 hours

    Dog friendly? Yes, off-leash

    Kid friendly? No

    Fees/Permits? None

    Best Season? Summer or Fall

Comment

Signal Peak (10,365 Ft) is the high point for both the Pine Valley Mountains and Washington County. The main route starts from the Oak Grove Campground and follows the trail up the South ridge very steeply before dropping into forested areas and then hiking off-trail to reach the summit.

This is a very dry hike, and you wouldn't want to hike this in the middle of summer because the temperatures in the St. George area can be extremely hot. The best time to hike this route is in fall, when the temperatures are cooler. You'll need to carry all your water for both you and the dogs. The nice thing about Signal Peak is there's nothing technical about it — dogs and humans can easily hike it, taking a full day to complete.

If you wanted to turn this into a quick overnight, there are plenty of campsites past mile 3; however, again, you would need to carry all of your own water.

Getting There

Heading south on I-15, you'll take exit 23 for Leeds, UT. Drive through the Silver Reef neighborhood, and eventually, the road turns to dirt. Turn right at the sign for Oak Grove Campground, and drive to the very end where the trail starts and the campground is. Small, compact cars should be able to make it as long as the road has been graded.

The Route

The trailhead starts from the campground. In the first 5 minutes, you'll see an unsigned trail split — stay right. You should be hiking west. You'll quickly come to the Pine Valley Mountain Wilderness/Dixie National Forest sign. After this sign, you'll hike up the first of many switchbacks. You'll see two blank posts and the trail now curves west again. It's never hard to lose the trail, but it does get quite brushy through all the oak (hence, the name oak grove). Wearing pants is highly recommended. After what seems like endless scrub oak and tiny switchbacks, you'll see a change of scenery as you start to climb in elevation and will see Spruce trees.

Once you reach the ridge, you'll drop down through a very forested area with some nice campsites. After you drop down the ridge and cut through the forested area, you'll approach the trail split sign from behind. Turn left (south), following the sign for "Further Water," which refers to the meadow ahead. Pass Deer Flat Meadow. Once again, you'll hike through a second forested area, and drop in elevation again. Hike past Further Water Meadow roughly 100 yards. Once you hike up that 100 yards or so, pick a comfortable place to start hiking off-trail. There's no official trail to the summit, and you may see cairns randomly placed. We followed the NE ridge the whole way.

Make sure you have a GPS or good map handy. I kept looking at my Gaia GPS to make sure we were hiking in the right direction. It's not super steep hiking up the ridge, there's no bushwhacking involved, and you can see through the trees pretty well. You won't be able to see the official summit until you get there. Reach the summit, somewhat hidden in trees but still marked by a summit register. From the summit, you can't see much since you are surrounded by trees.

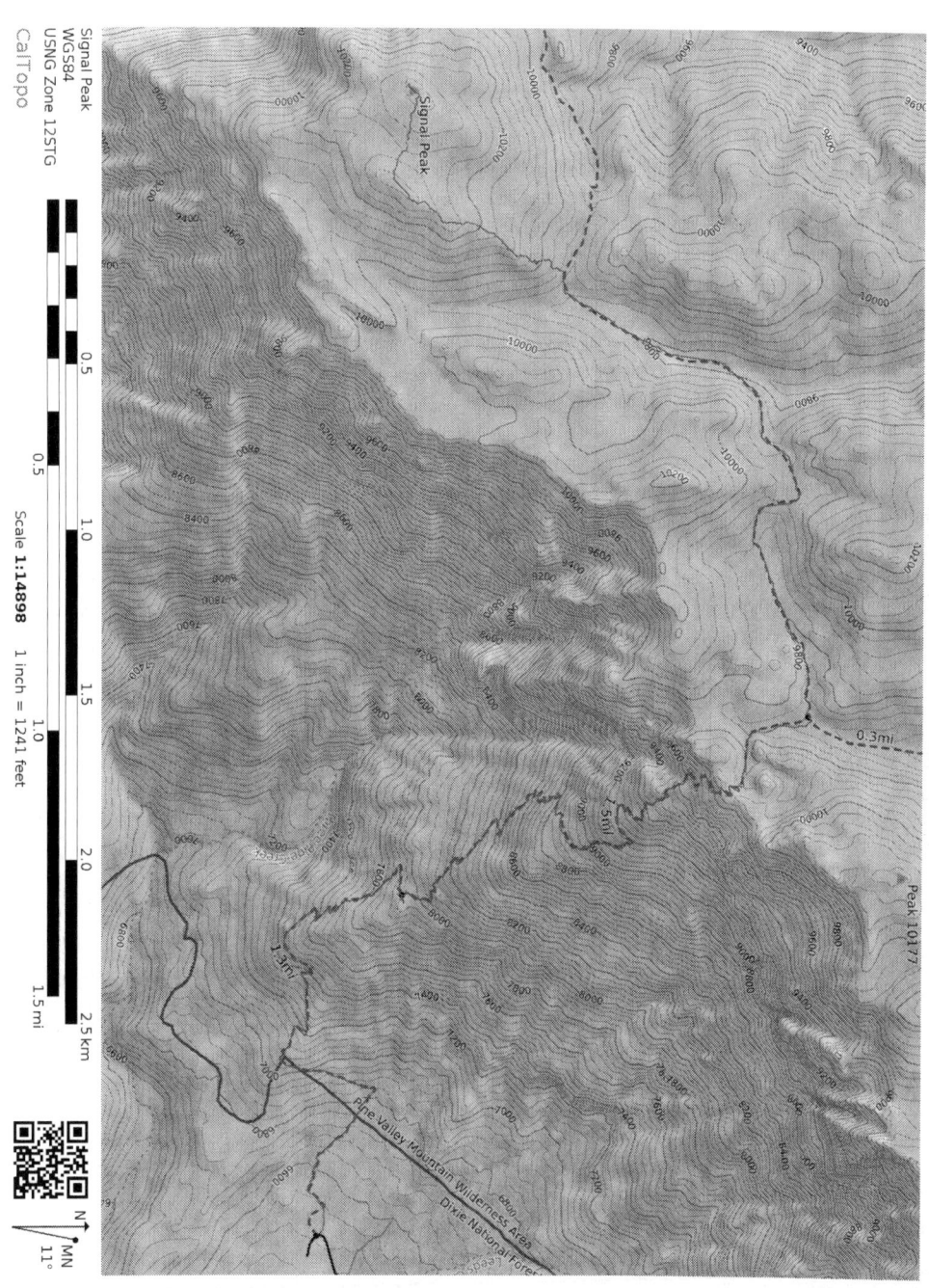

Monument Peak, Carbon County

Stats

Distance: n/a

Elevation gain: n/a

Driving Time: 1-2 hours RT
from HWY 264 turn off

Dog friendly? Yes, off-leash

Kid friendly? Yes, all ages

Fees/Permits? None

Best Season? Summer or Fall

Comment

Monument Peak (10, 452 Ft) is one of the easiest peaks since you can drive to the summit. It's located along the Wasatch Plateau, and because it's simply a drive, it should be combined with other CoHPs such as East Mountain and South Tent Mountain. There is nothing special about this peak except for the fact that you can see three CoHPs from the summit. The best time to drive here is in late summer to fall when the road is completely dry.

Getting There

From Spanish Fork, UT, head east on HWY 6, then turn south for US 89 for Fairview, UT. In Fairview, veer left for W 400 N on HWY 31. Drive 8.4 miles, and turn left at the brown sign for Electric Lake. Drive 10.6 miles and as you reach the saddle, look for the dirt road on your right. You will see a gate and the sign for FR018. Reset your odometer. Drive exactly 8 miles and look for the left turn. You can either park here and walk to the summit or continue driving if your car can make it. My Subaru Forester made it to the summit with no issues.

The Route

There is no hiking required; simply drive to the summit.

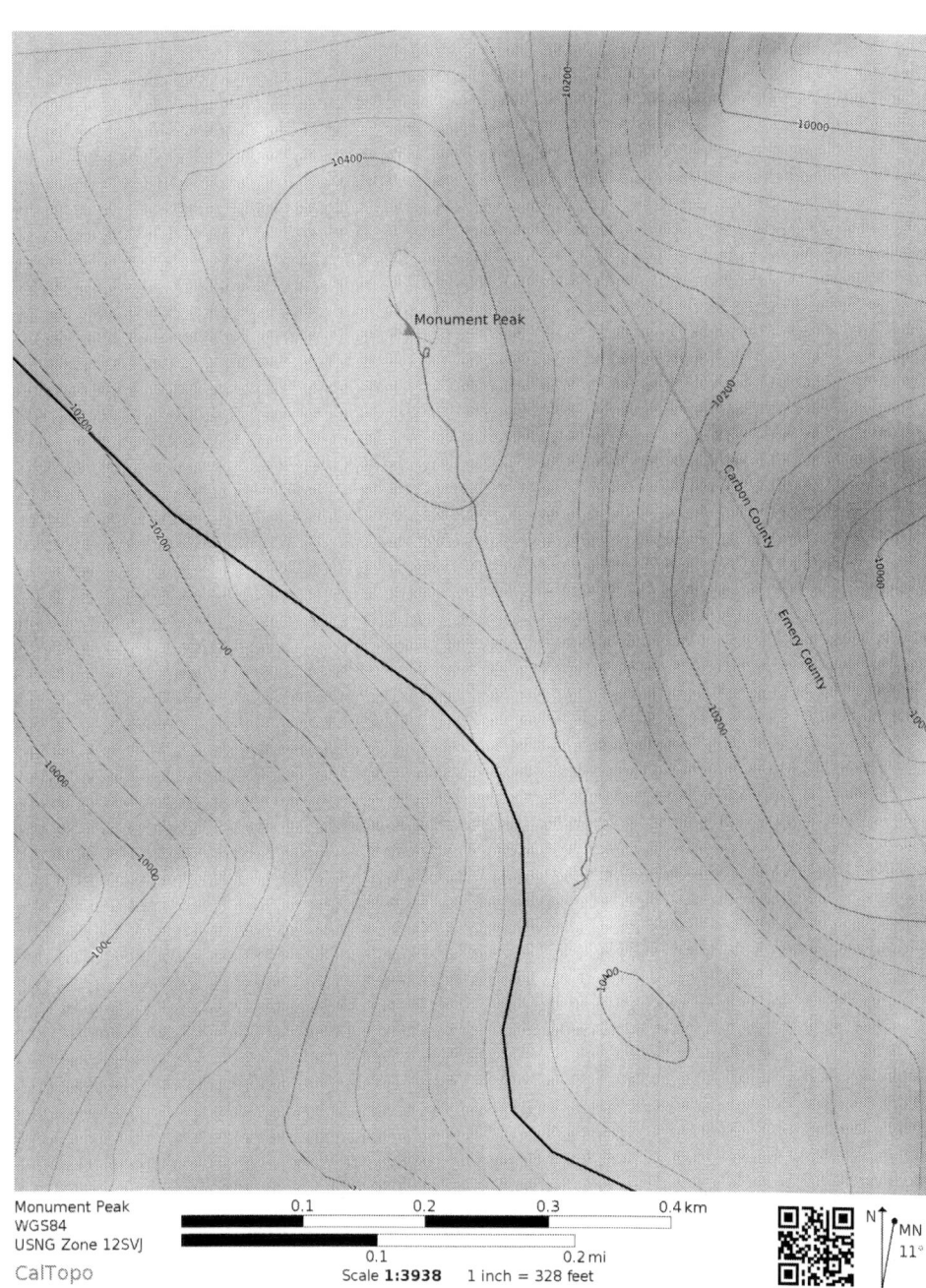

Monument Peak
WGS84
USNG Zone 12SVJ

CalTopo

Scale **1:3938**   1 inch = 328 feet

East Benchmark, Emery County

Stats

Distance: 4-6 miles RT
(depending on how far your
car can drive)
Elevation gain: 1,500 ft
Time: 2-4 hours
Dog friendly? Yes, off-leash
Kid friendly? Yes, ages 8+
Fees/Permits? None
Best Season? Summer or Fall

Comment

East Mountain (10, 743 Ft) is the Emery County High Point and is one of several peaks along the Wasatch Plateau. The hike itself is straight forward, following a well-worn trail used by horses, hunters, and hikers. It's one of the easier CoHPs and is often combined with Monument Peak, South Tent Mountain, or all three in one day. For our trip, we only did East & Monument on the same day since I had hiked South Tent Mountain a month earlier. From the summit, you can see three CoHPs. Camping is plentiful and the drive is scenic. Both dogs and older kids can hike this route.

Getting There

From Spanish Fork, UT, head East on HWY 6, then turn south for US 89 for Fairview, UT. In Fairview, veer left for W 400 N on HWY 31. Drive 18.2 miles. Just past the Huntington Reservoir, turn right on Miller Flat Road. You will now be on a well-graded dirt road and drive by numerous camping sites off the road. Drive 13 miles, and turn left at the signed Indian Creek Campground. Drive another mile, and turn left again, just after the cattle guard and another sign for Indian Creek Campground. Reset your odometer and drive 2 miles to the cattle guard.

The first mile is well graded; after that, you may need to park somewhere on this road and walk the rest of the way, depending on how bad the road is rutted. My Subaru Forester and zero issues reaching the gate. Once at the gate and small ATV cut-through, you can either park here and begin to hike, or if you can keep driving, unlock the barbed wire gate and continue driving 1 more mile to the end of the road and start hiking there.

We parked at and camped at the first cattle guard, only because I couldn't see at night that we could actually continue driving more. This is where we also began hiking.

The Route

If you parked at the first cattle gate, you'll need to walk the extra mile beyond this to the official trailhead. Hike up the small hill past the sign. Continue following the trail as it goes through a hallway of Aspen trees. At 1.3 miles (from the first cattle guard), the view opens and finally starts to gain elevation and works up one switchback. At 2.0 miles, you will reach the next trail split where the water troughs are. Stay right of the troughs. There is a trail split sign, but it's a little off to the left of where the main trail leads up. You'll want to stay hiking south (right).

This is where the Scad Valley Trail intersects if you take that route up instead. The trail really gets steep now. Keep an eye out for the last trail split at mile 2.1 to the right. We actually saw two Cow elk in this area! Keep following the trail as it heads south, and around 2.4 miles the trail fades away. It's not hard to know where to go though, just keep hiking up the hill to the South, mostly along the ridge. From the summit, you can see South & North Tent Mountain (the Sanpete County High Point)!

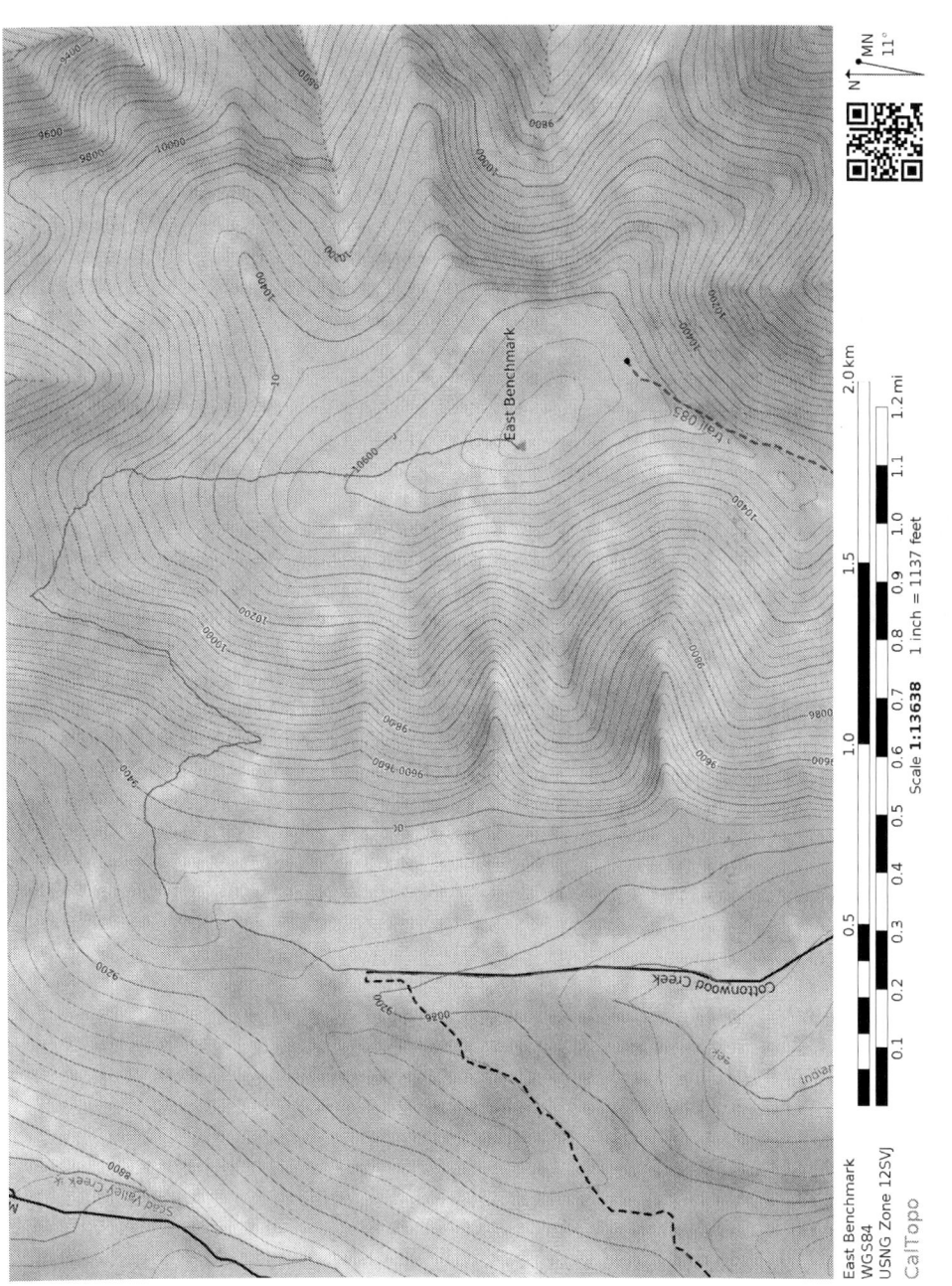

East Benchmark
WGS84
USNG Zone 12SVJ
CalTopo

Scale **1:13638**

1 inch = 1137 feet

Murdock Mountain-West Slope, Wasatch County

Stats

Distance: 2.5 miles RT

Elevation gain: 500 ft

Time: 1-2 hours

Dog friendly? Yes, off-leash

Kid friendly? Yes, if they're comfortable with small boulders

Fees/Permits? The Mirror Lake Highway charges a $6 fee for a 3-day pass. It's free if you have an annual Mirror Lake Hwy or American Fork Canyon pass, or free if you have an annual National Park Pass. No permit is required.

Best Season? Summer or Fall

Comment

Murdock West Slope (10,845 Ft) is the Wasatch County High Point and has no trail, but hiking through the boulder field is fairly easy and only 1 mile to reach. The views can't be beaten, and you're not likely to see people up there either.

Getting There

From Kamas, Utah, drive up the Mirror Lake Highway for 29 miles and turn left into the Bald Mountain TH/Picnic area.

The Route

Start from the Bald Mountain trailhead, then walk over to the summit from there. Walk along the road until you reach the Duchesne County sign, and start to hike right behind it. You'll hike through a forested section, but it's really easy to cut through to reach the ridge. From here, simply hike up in a straight line towards the ridge. The rocks are all small, so they're easier to step over. Keep your eye on your GPS to find the true summit, as there are cairns all over. You should have a great view of the Southeast.

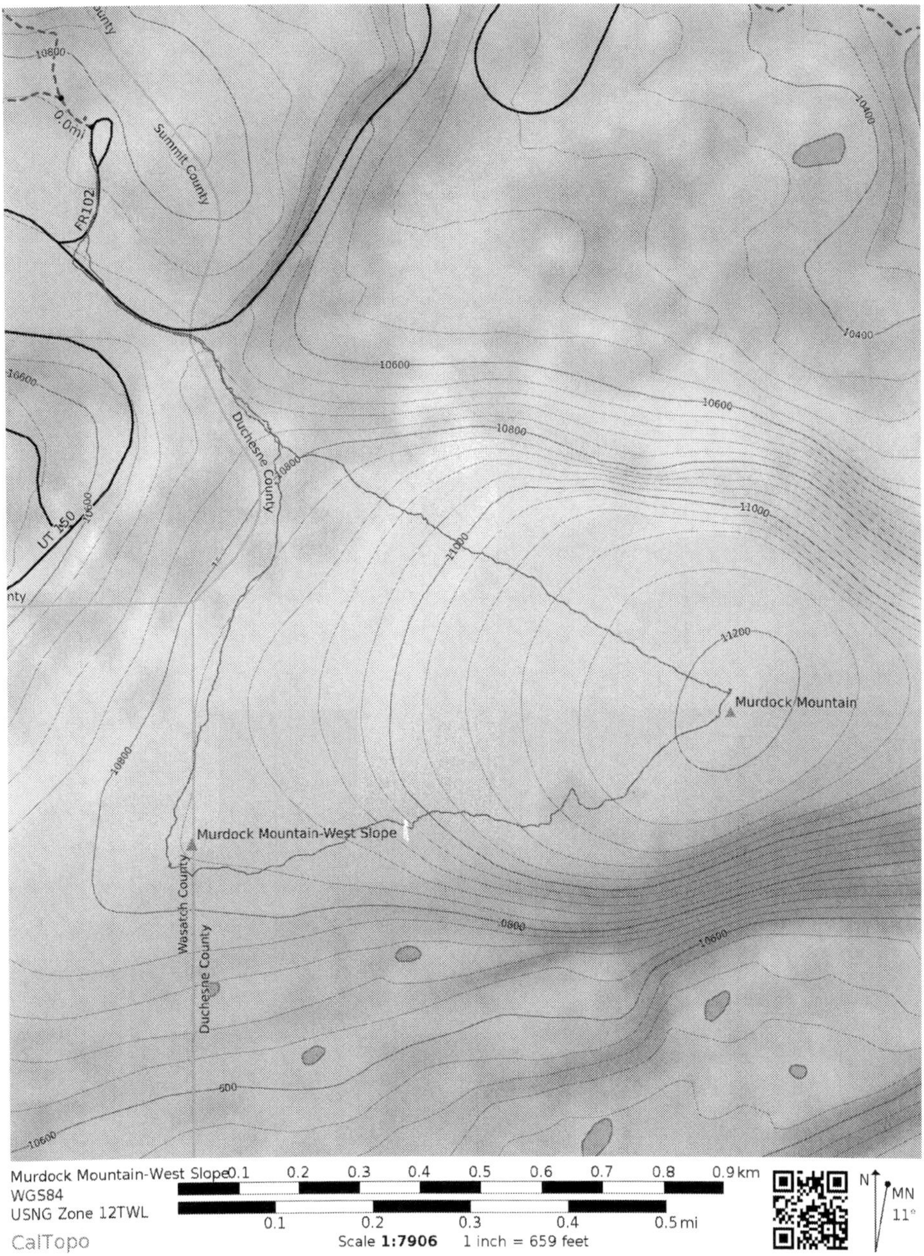

10600

Summit County

0.0mi

FR102

10600

UT 150

Duchesne County

10600

10600

10800

11000

11000

11200

10400

10600

11000

11200

Murdock Mountain

10800

Murdock Mountain-West Slope

Wasatch County

Duchesne County

10800

10800

10600

10600

10600

Murdock Mountain-West Slope
WGS84
USNG Zone 12TWL
CalTopo

0.1 0.2 0.3 0.4 0.5 0.6 0.7 0.8 0.9 km

0.1 0.2 0.3 0.4 0.5 mi

Scale **1:7906**   1 inch = 659 feet

N
MN
11°

Deseret Peak, Toole County

Stats

Distance: 9 miles RT (Loop)
Elevation gain: 3,700 ft
Time: 6-8 hours
Dog friendly? Yes, off-leash
Kid friendly? Ages 10+
　　depending on
　　peak-bagging experience
Fees/Permits? None
Best Season? Summer and Fall

Comment

Deseret Peak (11,031 Ft) is one of Utah's Ultra Prominent Peaks, is the tallest mountain in the Stansbury Mountain range, and the Tooele County highpoint. Therefore, this 9-mile loop is popular among peak baggers and those looking for an "easy" summit. This trail gains 3,700 Ft in just 4 miles, is dog friendly, and offers amazing views of the surrounding area.

The best time to hike here is typically June - November, or whenever the snow is mostly gone. However, you can still find patches of snow in June & July. While the valley can be in the 90s, Deseret Peak can still be very cold and windy on the summit. Bring plenty of water for you and your dogs. There is a stream at the beginning and end, but Charlie and I shared 3 liters of water between the two of us. Kids may be able to summit, depending on their peak bagging experience. I've even seen people carrying baby backpacks to the summit.

Getting There

From SLC, head west on I-80 and take exit 99 for Tooele, UT. Drive 3.4 miles, then turn right on HWY 138. Drive 10.8 miles and turn left on S. West St (you will also see a large brown sign for South Willow Canyon here). Drive 4.3 miles then turn right on S. Willow Drive for South Willow Canyon. Drive to the very end of the road to the trailhead. It's a dirt road, but well-graded. Any car can make it. There is a port-a-potty at the TH. The drive from SLC is about 1 hour 20 minutes.

The Route

The trail starts at the end of the road in S. Willow Canyon. You'll quickly pass the official Deseret Peak Wilderness sign. The trail gradually gains elevation for the first 2 miles. At 1.6 miles, you'll come to an unsigned trail split — stay left and cross the creek. This is the first and last good water stop for the dogs for the next 7 miles (until you return back down the loop). Across the creek is where you'll see the trail split, stay left. On your way back down the loop, you'll come in from the right. The last 1/2 mile leading up to the saddle starts to get steeper. You'll hike up several steep switchbacks. Once on the ridge, turn right and follow the well-traveled trail to the summit. Take time to enjoy the views from the summit. Work your way back down, creating a loop. Make sure you start hiking north to catch the trail down. Long switchbacks lead you down. Eventually, you'll make it to the next saddle before dropping down into the basin. Once again, you'll hike down long switchbacks. When you get to the next trail split, turn right. Going left will take you to South Willow Lake. Continue hiking your way back down the trail until you reach the same second trail split you initially passed, and make your way back to the trailhead.

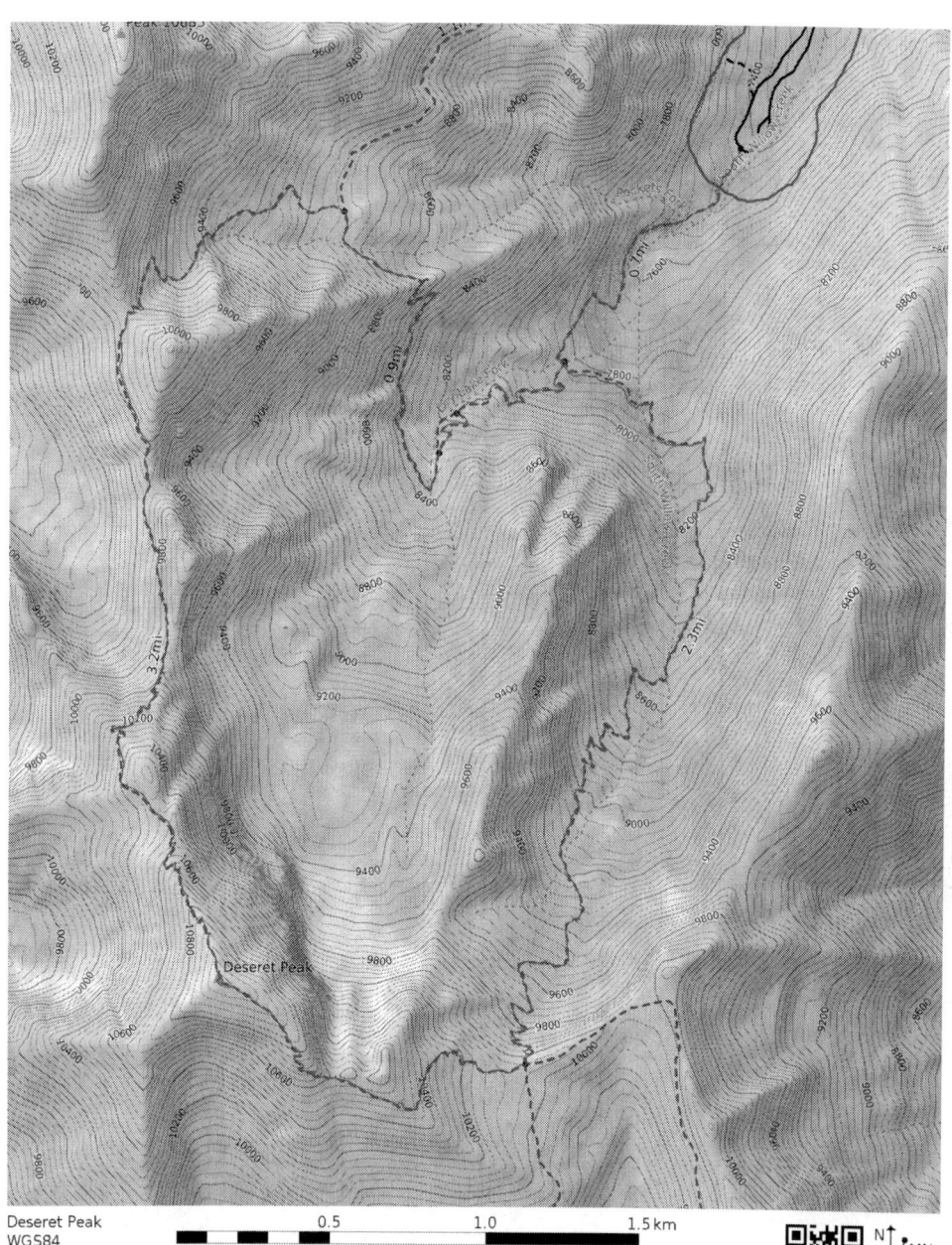

Deseret Peak
WGS84
USNG Zone 12TUK

CalTopo

Scale **1:15913**   1 inch = 1326 feet

South Tent Mountain, San Pete County

Stats

> Distance: 5 miles RT
> Elevation gain: 945 ft
> Time: 2-4 hours
> Dog friendly? Yes, off-leash
> Kid friendly? Yes, ages 9+
> Fees/Permits? None
> Best Season? Late Summer / Fall

Comment

South Tent Mountain (11,285 Ft) is the Sanpete County High Point and an amazing hike along a ridge with wide, open views the entire hike. Most people chose to hike south to north (on the South end of the mountain) and just aim for the South Tent saddle. However, we hiked the entire ridge to also bag North Tent Mountain (11,230 Ft). The ridge is a very easy hike, and no technical gear or scrambling is required. This route is only 5 miles RT - only a little longer than the traditional saddle route, yet you'll bag two peaks.

The hike itself has plenty of trees but is not well shaded. There is no water either, so you'll want to start hiking early in the day to beat the heat in the summer. The best months to access this mountain is July - September. The rest of the year, it has snow or the roads are completely muddy, making it impossible to even get near the trailhead. Make sure to bring at least 3 liters of water and plenty of sunblock — the sun seemed to be extra hot up here since there's no shade plus the elevation puts you closer to the sun.

Dogs should do well on this hike as long as they have experience hiking at least 5 miles and are used to high alpine terrain. Older kids (ages 9+) should also be able to hike this route.

Out of all the county high points, South Tent Mountain and the ridge is in my top five for views! I really loved this hike. Consider combining South Tent Mountain with East Mountain and Monument Peak (two other CoHPs).

Getting There

In Spring City, UT, head East on E 100 S. The road briefly turns left on S 700 E and then turns immediately onto Spring City Canyon Road. Follow this road up the canyon for 9 miles until it reaches Skyline Drive, and turn right. Drive one more mile, and veer left on FR2203. Drive down about 100 yards or until you find a good spot to turn around and park. Begin hiking here.

The Route

Park near the end of the ridge (the northernmost area), where the road splits off a little, and start hiking from there. Begin hiking towards the ridge. There's no trail for this section; just aim up as you reach the lower section of the ridge catch the faint trail. After hiking up the ridge and following the faint trail, come to a first really nice overlook. That road below is the road most people continue driving to reach the popular starting point for this peak. Continue following the ridge. After only 1.2 miles summit North Tent Mountain. From North Tent Mountain, simply follow the ridge down to the saddle (again, that is the area where most people hike up to, coming up from the right side of this photo). South Tent Mountain is the peak ahead and your destination. Again, catch a faint trail the entire hike along the ridge. Just stay on the ridge, and you should be aiming for South Tent Mountain. Sign the summit register, then returned the same way you hiked up, along the NW ridge.

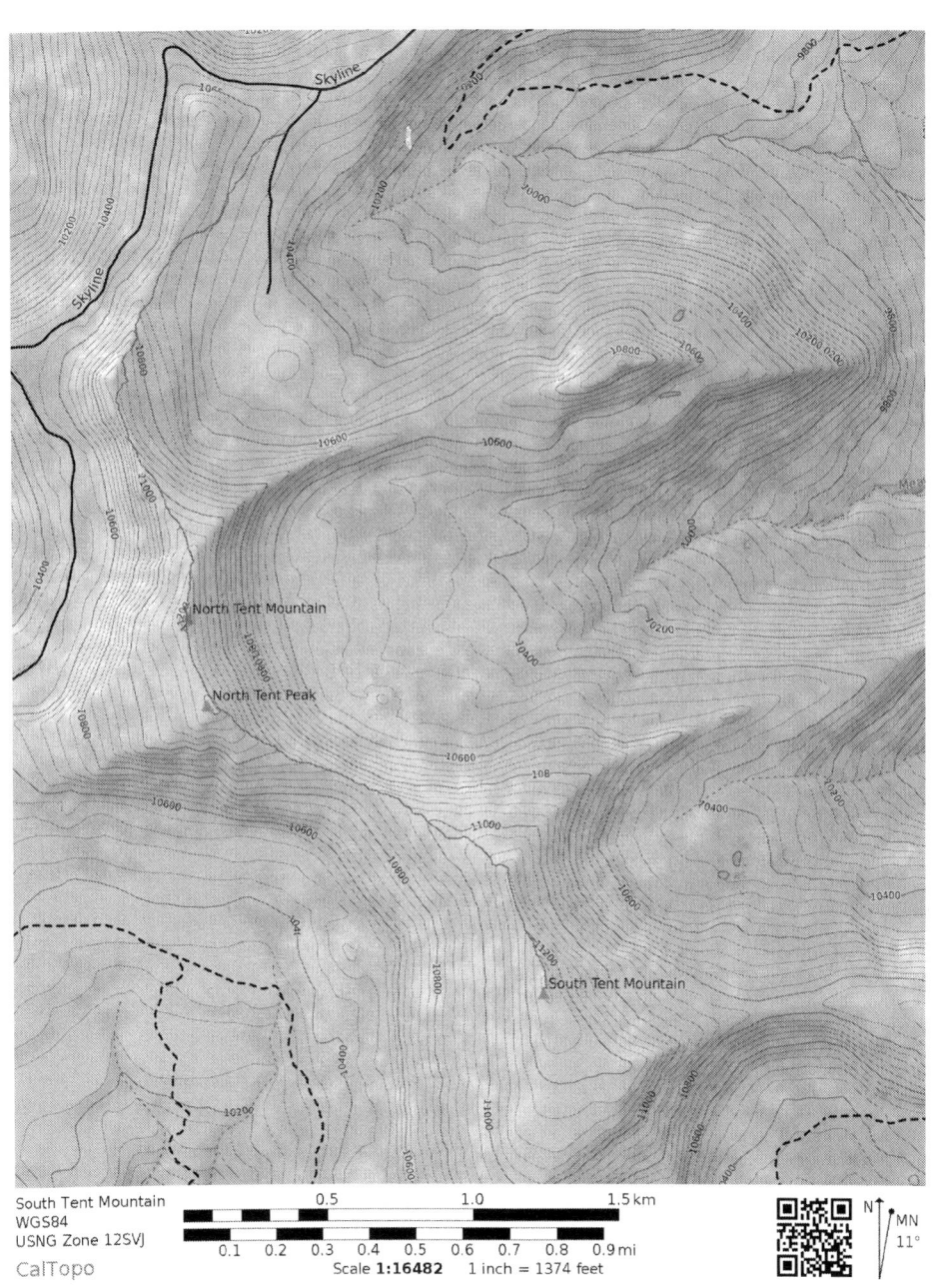

South Tent Mountain
WGS84
USNG Zone 12SVJ
CalTopo

Scale **1:16482**   1 inch = 1374 feet

Brian Head Peak, Iron County

Stats

Distance: n/a

Elevation gain: n/a

Time: 10 minutes RT

Dog friendly? Yes, off-leash

Kid friendly? Yes!

Fees/Permits? None

Best Season: Summer & Fall

Comment

Brian Head Peak (11,307ft) is the Iron County High Point and is located at Brian Head Ski Resort. There is no hiking, but rather a very casual walk to the summit that even kids can do. It's a great place to take visitors and tourists to "bag" a peak they can literally drive to and have amazing views of the area. The gate to drive to the summit is typically open June through October or whenever it's free of snow and dry. Even in summer, the temperatures can be quite chilly at that high of an elevation. Bring a light jacket and a camera, and check out the views!

Getting There

From I-15 near Parowan, UT take exit 78, then left on Main St. Turn left on E. Center St, then this turns into S. Canyon Rd. Follow this for about 14.5 miles, through Brian Head Ski Resort. Past the resort, look for the brown sign for Vista Overlook, and the dirt road turns right leading up to the peak. Drive this dirt road to the very end, at Brian Head Peak. This road is typically only from June - October. If the gate is closed, you will need to hike up the 3 miles to the peak.

The Route

This is one of the few CoHPs that doesn't require a hike. Simply drive to the summit.

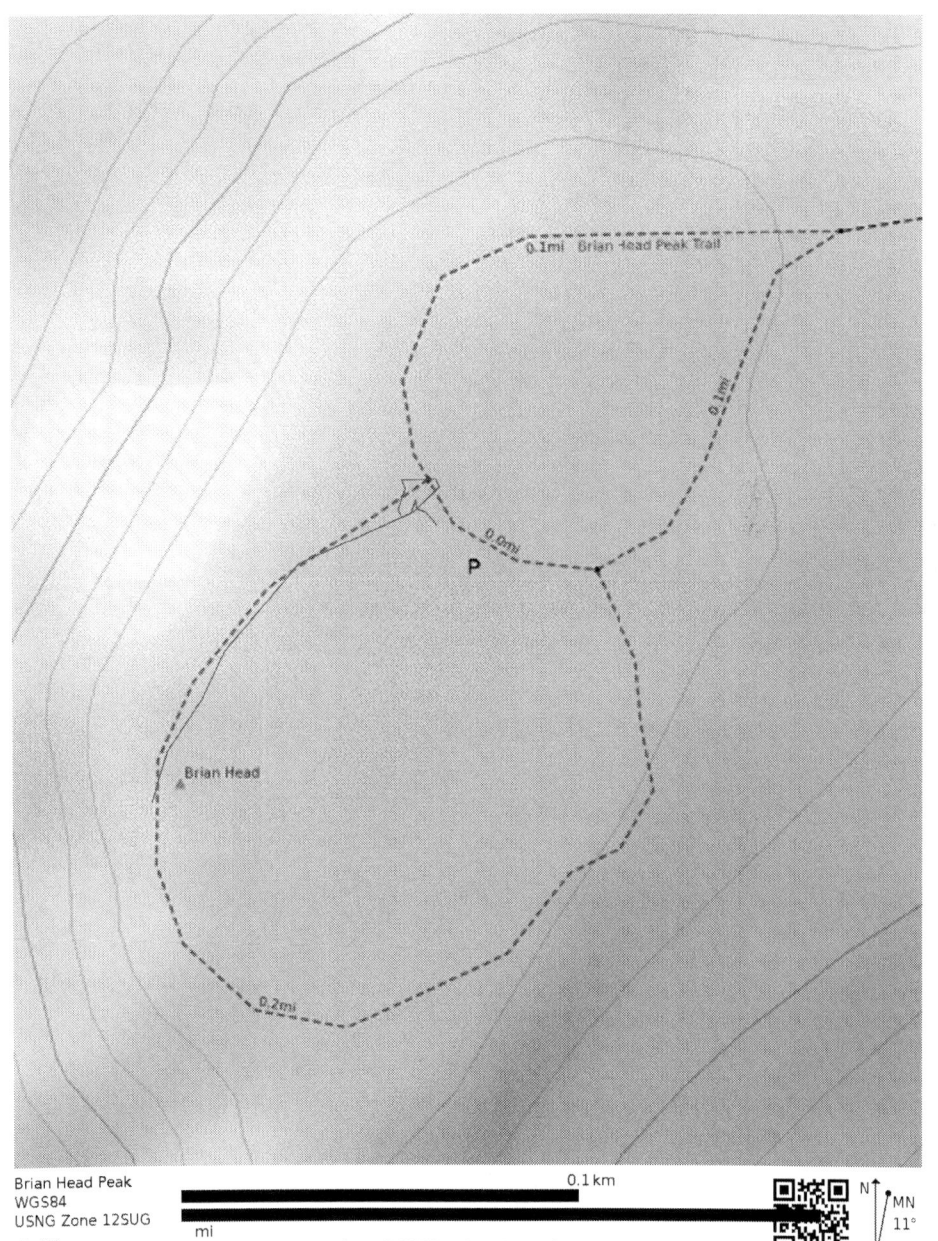

0.1mi Brian Head Peak Trail

0.1mi

0.0mi

P

Brian Head

0.2mi

Brian Head Peak
WGS84
USNG Zone 12SUG

CalTopo

0.1 km

mi

Scale **1:1201** 1 inch = 100 feet

N
MN
11°

Bluebell Knoll, Wayne County

Stats

Distance: 0.4 miles RT

Elevation gain: 75 ft

Time: 15-20 minutes

Dog friendly? Yes, off-leash

Kid friendly? Yes

Fees/Permits? None

Best Season? Summer & Fall

Comment

Boulder Top (aka Bluebell Knoll) sits at 11,322 ft high on the Aquarius Plateau, in-between Loa, Utah and Boulder, Utah. It's not a hike, but rather a scenic drive with about a 10-minute walk to the summit, which sits in a grove of forested trees, yet also has a view of the nearby Raft Lake just below the summit. Boulder Top is the name for the area, and Bluebell Knoll is the official summit name, but Utah locals use both names synonymously. Because this CoHP isn't a hike, it's good to combine this trip with other nearby CoHPs, such as Fish Lake High Top. This area is great for the whole family, and the best time to visit is in late summer to fall when the roads are dry, gates are open, and the leaves are bursting in color.

Getting There

From Loa, UT head south on HWY 24, through the towns of Bicknell, UT and Lyman, UT. Turn right on Bicknell Circle (also called the Fish Hatchery Road). Stay on this road as it turns to dirt, following signs for Bluebell Knoll, and the road turns into FR178. 3 miles before Bluebell Knoll will be a gate. This is a good place to park a small car and either jump in a friend's 4x4 car OR walk to the TH if you don't have a high clearance car. This gate is only open typically June through October or when the snow is all gone and dry. Call the ranger station to make sure it's open before making the trip down. From the gate, continue the last 3 miles to reach Bluebell Knoll's sign on your left (north).

The Route

You'll pass a brown sign that says Bluebell know is 2 miles. From the last gate, it's about 3 miles to the summit. Past that gate, you'll want a higher clearance car. I wouldn't have felt comfortable taking my Forester up there, to give you an idea. A jeep or truck will be best. You'll see the official sign right off the road, but now it's time to "hike." After a 10 minute walk aiming for the top, we found the official summit cairn.

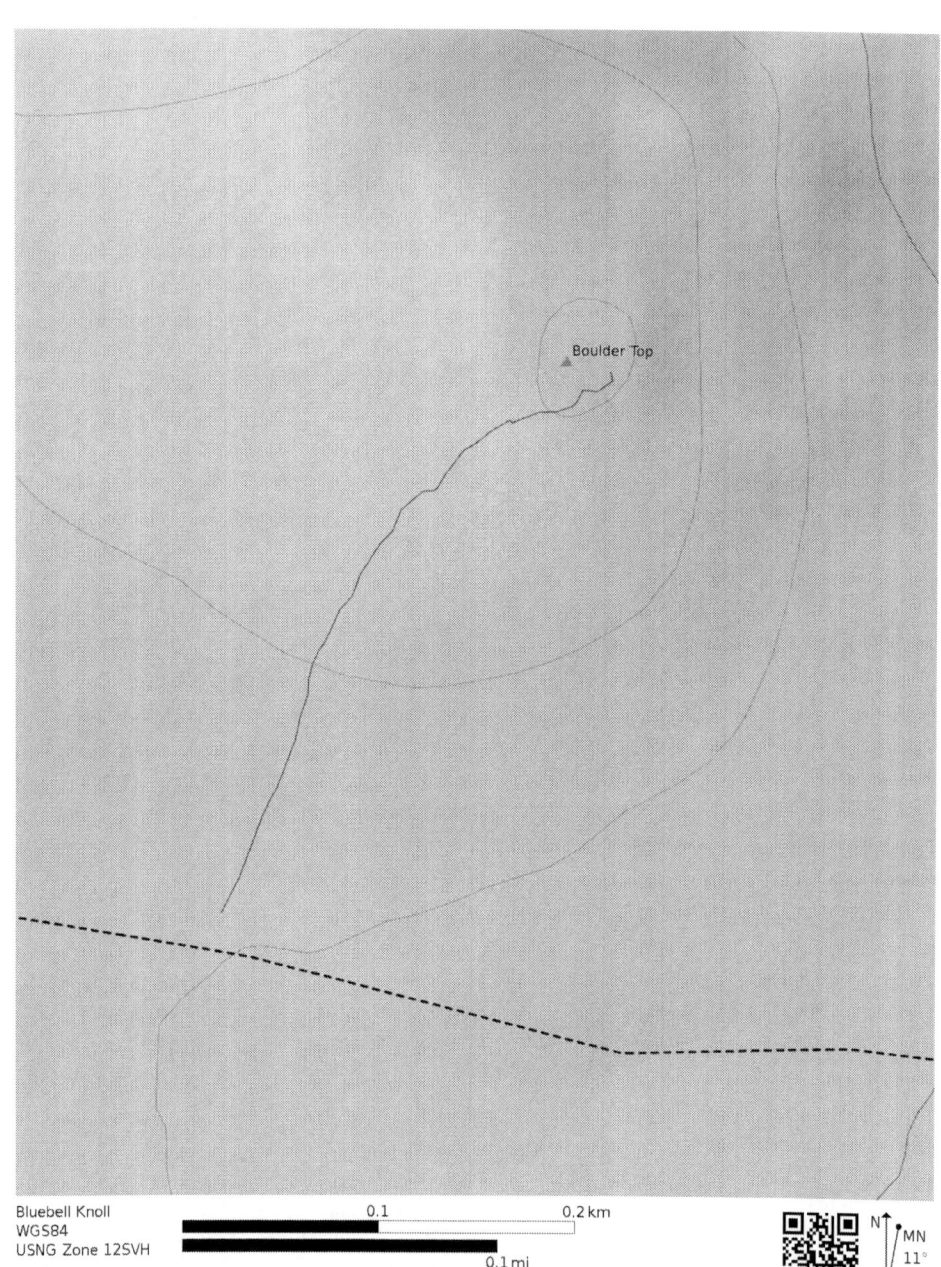

Bluebell Knoll
WGS84
USNG Zone 12SVH

0.1   0.2 km

0.1 mi

CalTopo   Scale **1:2469**   1 inch = 206 feet

N MN 11°

American Fork Twin Peaks, Salt Lake County

Stats

Distance: 2.2 miles (RT)

Elevation gain: 960 ft

Time: 2-3 hours

Dog friendly? No, LCC is part of the watershed, so dogs are not allowed in any part of the canyon.

Kid friendly? No

Fees/Permits: If you take the Snowbird tram, each ticket is $20; no permit needed

Best Season? Summer & Fall

Comment

Hiking to the American Fork Twin Peaks (11,490 Ft) is not for the beginner hiker. This route leads hikers across a long knife edge with a very faint trail. Do not attempt this hike if you've never crossed a very narrow and rocky ridgeline before — it takes a little route finding, skill, no fear of heights, and requires some light scrambling. Gloves are useful for this hike, so they provide extra grip and protection from the sharp rocks.

Getting There

To get to Snowbird from SLC, drive east on I-80, then take I-215 south. Take exit 6 for Wasatch Blvd, and head East/South. Follow this road, past Big Cottonwood Canyon (south past the 7-11). You'll drive past a few lights, and the road will naturally curve into Little Cottonwood Canyon. Drive-up LCC for about 8 miles until you see the sign for the Snowbird Aerial Tram. After you park, continue following signs as you walk towards the ticket office and take the ridge's tram. Restrooms, food, water, and emergency services are available at the Tram Lodge.

The most popular trail to AF Twin Peaks starts from Snowbird Ski Resort. My friend and I took the "easy" way to the trailhead, which allowed us to tram up to the ridge line and then hike the 1 mile to the first summit. The other (free) route is starting from the base of the resort and hiking all the way up to the peak.

Starting from the base of Snowbird would require about a 4-6 hour hike (round trip), while taking the tram only requires about a 2-3 hour hike (round trip). Many experienced Peak Baggers may scoff at you for taking the tram up, then hiking to the summit, but being able to cross the knife edge is a feat in itself!

This hike is definitely NOT suited for beginner hikers nor beginner peak baggers. I highly recommend that you have a few summits under your belt (with knife edges) before attempting this route, and you should be comfortable on sheer drop-offs. I also recommend that you take a hiking buddy along to help motivate and assist you with the awkward maneuvers needed on some parts of the ridge.

The Route

Once you get off the tram, continue straight down the steep dirt road past the ski lift. At the small hill, hike up past three small ski signs. Starting out, there is a faint trail for the first 100 yards on the ridge. Reach your first obstacle — scrambling over or around boulders with trees blocking the way. At the narrowest, the knife-

edge is only about 1 foot wide. There are 3 main sections of the trail, as I will be referring to. The white rocks (1st section), black rocks (2nd section), and the summit trail (3rd section). The 1st section is the hardest, with the most awkward and hard-to-maneuver scrambles. From this point, you can clearly see the black rocks. It looks much steeper than where you are currently hiking, but trust me, ridges and summits always look worse than they actually are. If you feel shaky or scared, just take it really slow across this 1st section (white rocks). You'll see some faint trails and footprints going in every direction, but I highly recommend that you stay as close to the ridge as possible. Every time you start you head down, you'll have to hike back up - conserve your energy and just stay as high as possible. Section 3 (summit trail), has loose rock. Make sure you wear shoes with really good tread. Reach the summit. Head back the same way you came. If you have time, hike over to some of the surrounding peaks to get more awesome views. Keep in mind that the last tram leaves the ridge at 8 pm, so plan accordingly.

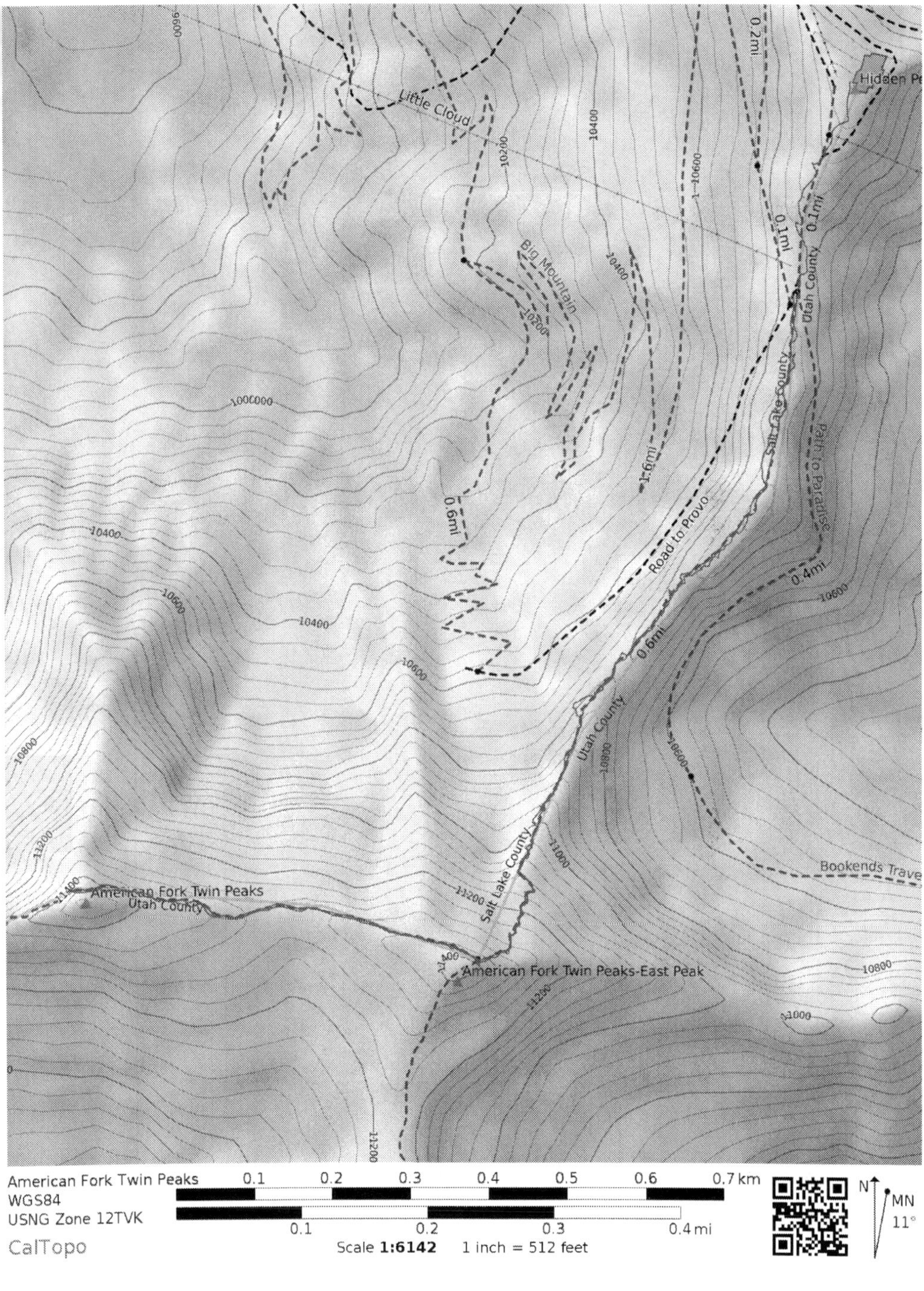
Little Cloud
Big Mountain
Hidden Pe
0.2mi
0.1mi
0.1mi
Utah County
Salt Lake County
Path to Paradise
Road to Provo
1.6mi
0.6mi
0.4mi
0.6mi
Utah County
Salt Lake County
Bookends Trave
American Fork Twin Peaks
Utah County
American Fork Twin Peaks-East Peak
10200
10400
10600
10800
11000
11200
American Fork Twin Peaks
WGS84
USNG Zone 12TVK
CalTopo
0.1 0.2 0.3 0.4 0.5 0.6 0.7 km
0.1 0.2 0.3 0.4 mi
Scale 1:6142 1 inch = 512 feet
N
MN
11°

Mt.Ellen, Garfield County

Stats

Distance: 5.8 miles RT

Elevation gain: 1,024 ft

Time: 3-5 hours

Dog friendly? Yes, off-leash

Kid friendly? Yes, older kids with
   hiking experience

Best season? Summer & Fall

Comment

Mount Ellen (11,522 Ft) & Mt. Ellen Peak (11,506 Ft) are in the Henry Mountains, about 45 minutes - 1 hour south of Hanksville, UT. The Henry Mountains are an island of a sort, as they are surrounded by three of Utah's National Parks - Capital Reef, Arches, and Canyonlands. Mount Ellen is a hulk of a mountain, composed of two distinct parts. The first is the North Ridge, which has the 3 highest summits in the Henry's.

At the far northern end of the ridge is the pyramid-shaped peak called Mt.Ellen Peak. At times in the past and during early mapping expeditions, it was used as a campsite where geologists took triangulation measurements by & for the USGS. On top are several old tent platforms. The highest peak, however, is the peak just before Mt. Ellen Peak, called Mount Ellen. The second distinct part is the South Ridge, which includes the mining area known as Bromide Basin. The highest point is what I refer to as South Ridge Peak and has an old and now-unused solar-powered radio tower on top.

The trailhead for Mount Ellen & Mt. Ellen Peak starts from Bull Creek Pass - driving up this dirt road is best suited for a high clearance car. We did have one Outback Subaru drive, but got a flat tire. Our Jeep Wrangler and Toyota Tacoma made it just fine. The road is randomly grated and requires crossing a few creeks.

There is a campground on BLM0095 called Lonesome Beaver. Camping is primitive, so you will need to bring your own water. There are no restrooms or fees.

Getting There

From Hanksville, drive south on HWY 95 for 10.4 miles. Turn right onto the dirt road, BLM0095. Stay on this as it turns into Granite Road. Once you reach Sawmill Basin Road (at the "T), turn left. Follow this road as it again turns into BLM0095, and follow the signs for Bull Creek Pass to where the trail starts.

The Route

The trail to Mount Ellen is well defined, and you can clearly see your first destination — sometimes, the trail cuts over a rocky path. Near the ridgeline, you will lose the trail. Just continue following the ridge, up and over the small boulder fields. The rocks aren't big enough that you have to jump or wear scrambling gloves, but be wary of where you step — most rocks are unstable. Reach Mount Ellen. To get to Mt. Ellen Peak, continue along the ridge for another 3/4 mile. The trail drops about 400 Ft; then you have to hike back up to the peak. Mt. Ellen Peak is only 14 Ft lower in elevation compared to Mount Ellen. It looks close, but it's deceiving! Make our way up the small switchbacks.

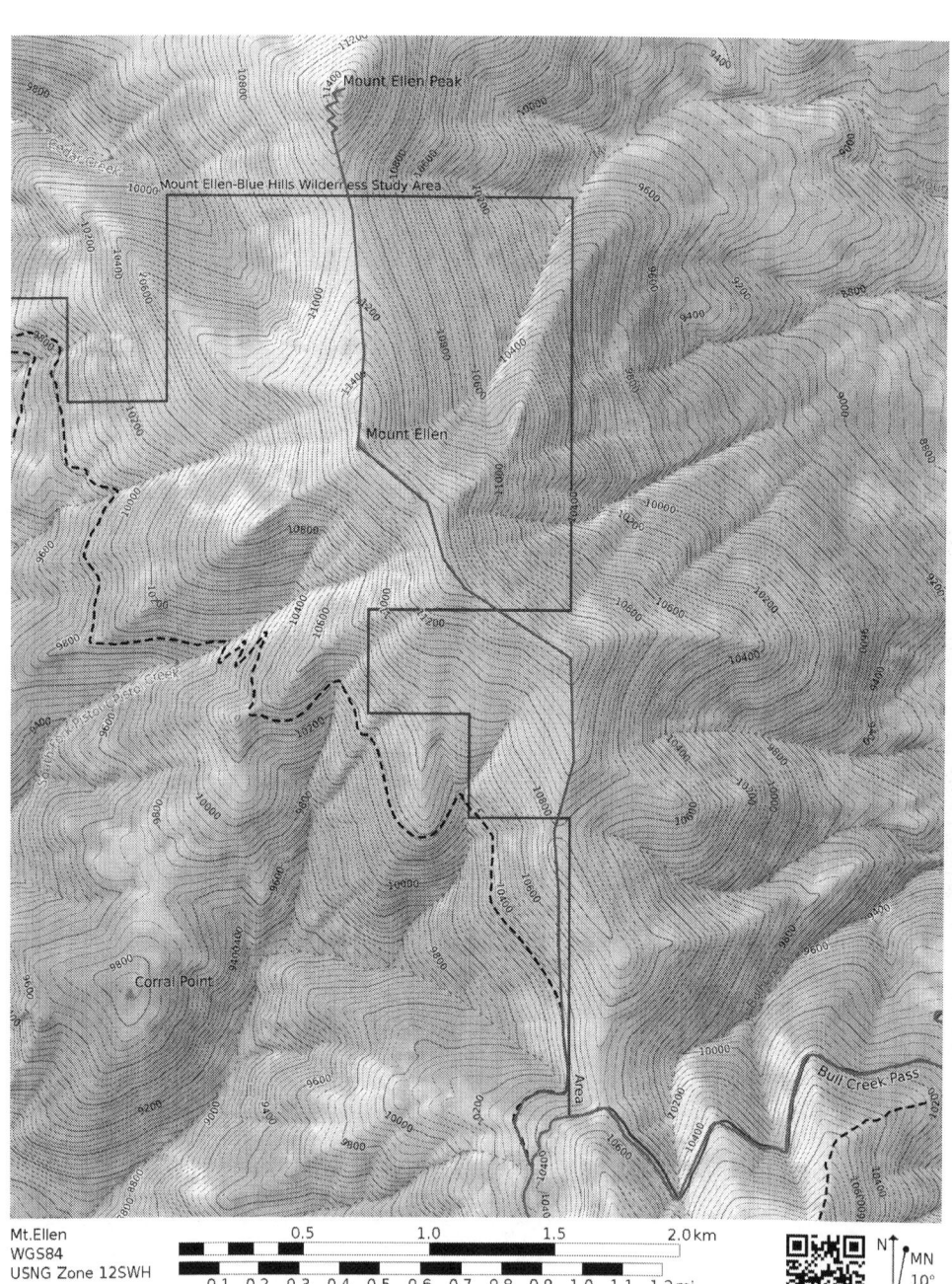

Fish Lake Hightop, Sevier County

Stats

Distance: 9 miles RT

Elevation gain: 2,400 ft

Time: 5-7 hours

Dog friendly? Yes, off-leash

Kid friendly? Yes, ages 9+

Fees/Permits? None

Best season? Summer or Fall

Comment

Fish Lake Hightop (11,633 Ft) is the Sevier County High Point. The trail itself follows Pelican Canyon for 4.5 miles, gradually gaining elevation. The lower half of the hike is very shaded and earlier in the year Pelican Canyon Creek flows; however, come fall it is typically dry. The upper half is much more exposed and works up a few steep hills and small switchbacks before reaching the plateau. Once on the plateau, you can clearly see your destination, Fish Lake High Top. Plenty of camping is available all around Fish Lake.

Getting There

From Salina, UT, drive south on HWY 24. Turn left at the signed "Fish Lake". Drive 10 miles, then turn left on FR034/Pelican Overlook. Park at the end of the road. High clearance is needed to reach the overlook. If you only have a small car, you'll need to park lower then walk up to the TH.

The Route

The trail begins at Pelican Point (aka Promontory) at the East end of Fish Lake. Start by hiking past the official sign at an old wood fence. Within the first two minutes, you'll reach the first trail split. There is no sign (just a wood stick), but stay left. At 0.5 mile, keep straight/right up the canyon. Turning left takes you down to the Bowery Resort & Campground. The hill begins to get steeper but still shaded. Parts of it are rocky. At mile 2.3 miles, reach another trail split. Stay right this time. Just off to the left is a pond. It's pretty mucky, but the dogs didn't mind since they could cool off for a minute. There were also very old cabin remnants near here as well. Now the next mile goes up more steep hills but also through flat meadows. The trail fades a little near the top but is well marked by large cairns. Eventually, about 1/2 mile from the summit, we saw a large brown sign. It only shows an inaccurate map, so we kept hiking, this time aiming for the actual summit to the North. Hike up through some boulders to reach the top, keeping an eye on your GPs for the true summit.

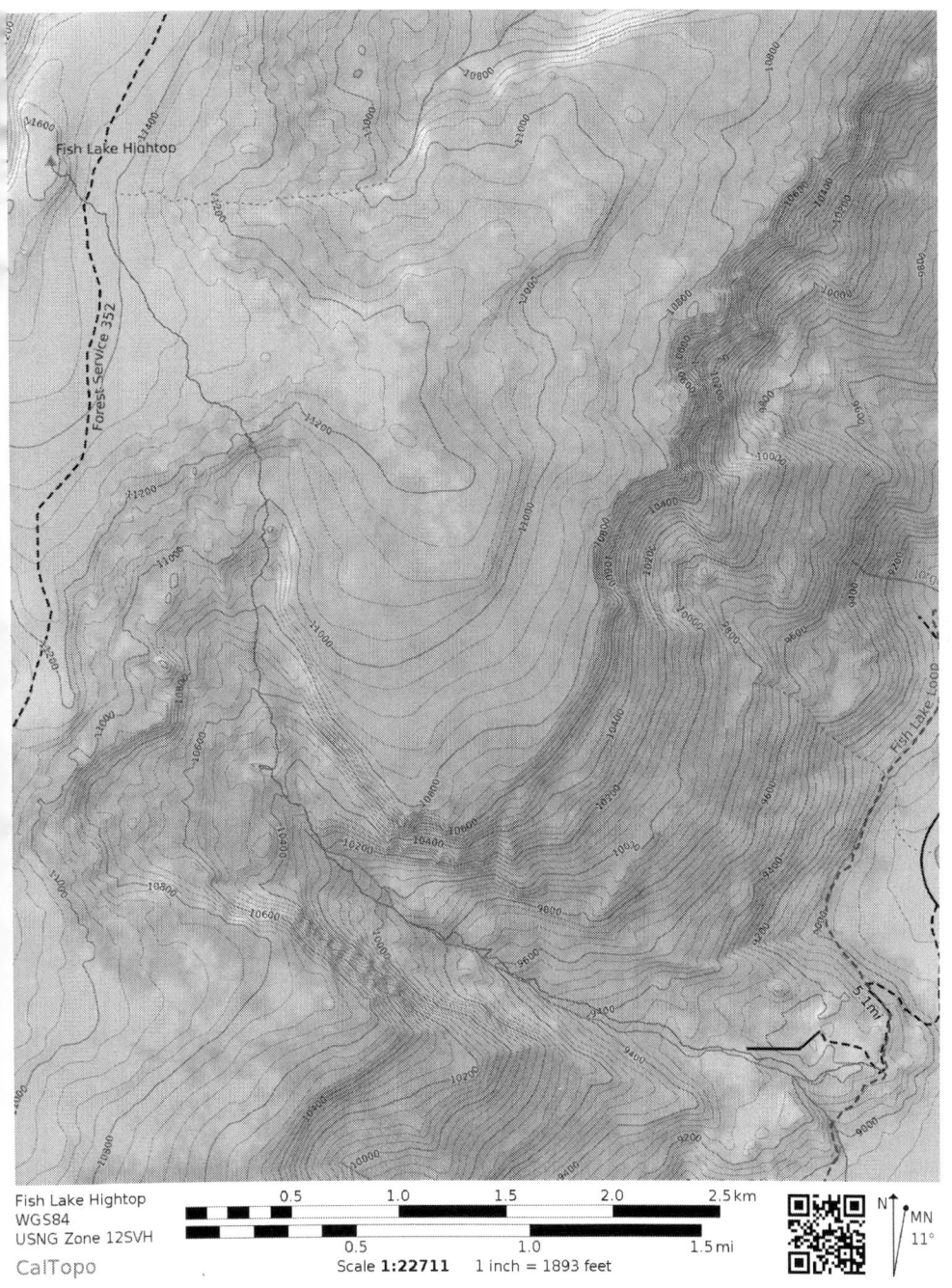

Fish Lake Hightop
WGS84
USNG Zone 12SVH

CalTopo

Scale **1:22711**   1 inch = 1893 feet

Mt. Nebo, Utah County

Stats

Distance: 9 miles round trip

Elevation gain: 3600 Ft

Time: 6-8 hours

Dog friendly? Yes, off-leash

Kid friendly? No

Best season? Summer & Fall

Comment

Mt. Nebo (11,929 Ft) is the highest peak in the Wasatch Mountains and Utah County. Mt. Nebo actually has two summits, the North and south, with the North being the higher of the two. This is a popular hike, so the trail is well maintained and easy to follow. Around 9,000 Ft, a bench trail runs level north to south, as it reaches Wolf Pass. From there, the trail steadily climbs to a false summit before reaching the ridge that leads to the true summit. This is a strenuous yet very rewarding hike, as you can see for several miles around.

Getting There

From SLC, drive south on I-15 towards Payson, UT, and take exit 250 for Main St. At the first light, turn Left onto E 100 N. At the next light, turn right onto the Nebo Loop Road. Brown signs are pointing you in the right direction. Once you turn onto the Nebo Loop Road, drive about 25 miles to the signed Monument Trailhead parking area. As soon as you turn into the lot, turn right onto Mona Drive, and park at the end of this road.

The Route

Start by following the cattle fence, and hike past an old sign. This 1st mile is the easiest and very gradual. Work your way up and through a meadow. This is where the trail really starts to get hard once you reach the ridge. Reach Wolf Pass. This is a great spot to take a snack break and prepare yourself for climbing to the false peak. After summiting the false peak, continue along the ridge. This ridge scares a lot of people; however, the trail is really well defined & traveled. It's wide, and there's no chance of falling. Reach the North summit of Mt.Nebo.

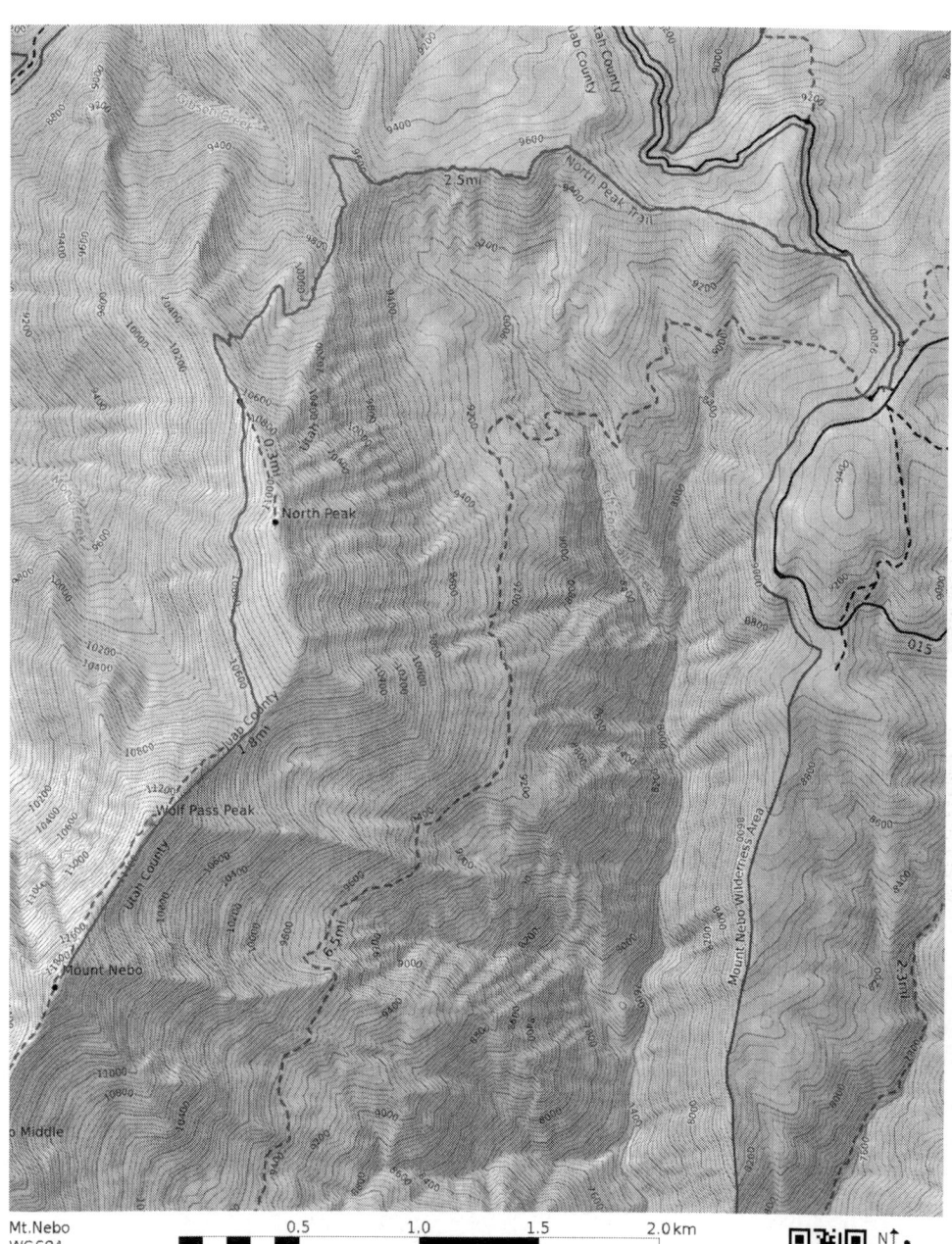

Mt.Nebo
WGS84
USNG Zone 12SVK
CalTopo

Scale **1:20511**   1 inch = 1709 feet

MN
11°

Ibapah Peak, Juab County

Stats

Distance: 14-18 miles round trip
(depending on how far you can
drive up)
Elevation gain: 5,900 ft
Time: 12-14 hours
Dog friendly? Yes, off-leash
Kid friendly? No
Best season? Late summer or Fall

Comment

Ibapah Peak is the tallest point in the Deep Creek Mountains and Juab County, at 12,087 Ft. This peak is often considered the hardest CoHP. Getting to to the trailhead is a long drive since it's about a 4-hour drive from SLC. The Deep Creeks are truly a unique place in the West Desert. The long-distance from the major population allows hikers to find solitude. The desert at the foot of the mountain is at an elevation of about 4,800 Ft, giving the mountains an enormous vertical rise of 7,300 ft - greater than that of the famous Teton's in Wyoming. Plan on camping near the TH the day before you hike here - camping is free, and there are a few spots that already have a fire ring. You'll want to have an early start to your hike and be prepared to give your legs a workout.

Getting There

Head west on I-80 towards Wendover, NV. Take exit 410 in Wendover for US-93. Turn left at the 1st light, then right onto US-93. Drive for 25.6 miles and look for a sign for Ibapah Road and turn left. Stay on this and drive past the tiny town of Gold Hill, UT. This road turns into the Pony Express-Overland Stage Trail Road. Past Callao, UT, turn right onto the "Deep Creek Mtns Road" for about 13 miles, where you'll see a sign for the Granite Creek Road. Follow this road for 4.3 miles to the trailhead. You'll need a high clearance car for this area. Drive up as far as you can, or until you see a possible campsite.

The Route

Start by walking up the dirt road past your campsite. You'll see smooth looking rocks on your right. When you pass a gate, that's where the "trail" starts, but it's still an old jeep road for the next 2 miles. You'll cross a stream right around the corner from here. After the jeep road ends, and turns into a trail, keep an eye out for a cairn to your left. You don't want to miss this, or you won't go the right way. Cross over another stream bed, then catch the trail again. Now the trail gets steep and will stay this way the rest of the hike. You'll cut through lots of sagebrush on this trail. We came to a small meadow and had a great view of Red Mountain. Red Mountain is another peak you can summit, and the elevation is only about 500 ft lower in elevation compared to Ibapah. However, the quartzite-clad Red Mountains provide a cool visual counterbalance to the white granite face of Ibapah Peak. Reach the large open, dry meadow. This is a great place to take a rest and snack break. You are only halfway there.

From this meadow, you will want to cut straight across in a northerly direction and work your way to the sub-peak. There is no trail from this point - just route finding. Reach the sub peak base, and just around the corner to the left is the saddle. When you work your way from the sub-peak to the saddle, you'll see the trail come and go. Sometimes you'll be on the sides of rock walls; however, they are totally doable — even Charlie could cut across them. Once you pass the saddle, you'll find a well-defined trail. From here, it's an "easy" 900 Ft to the summit.

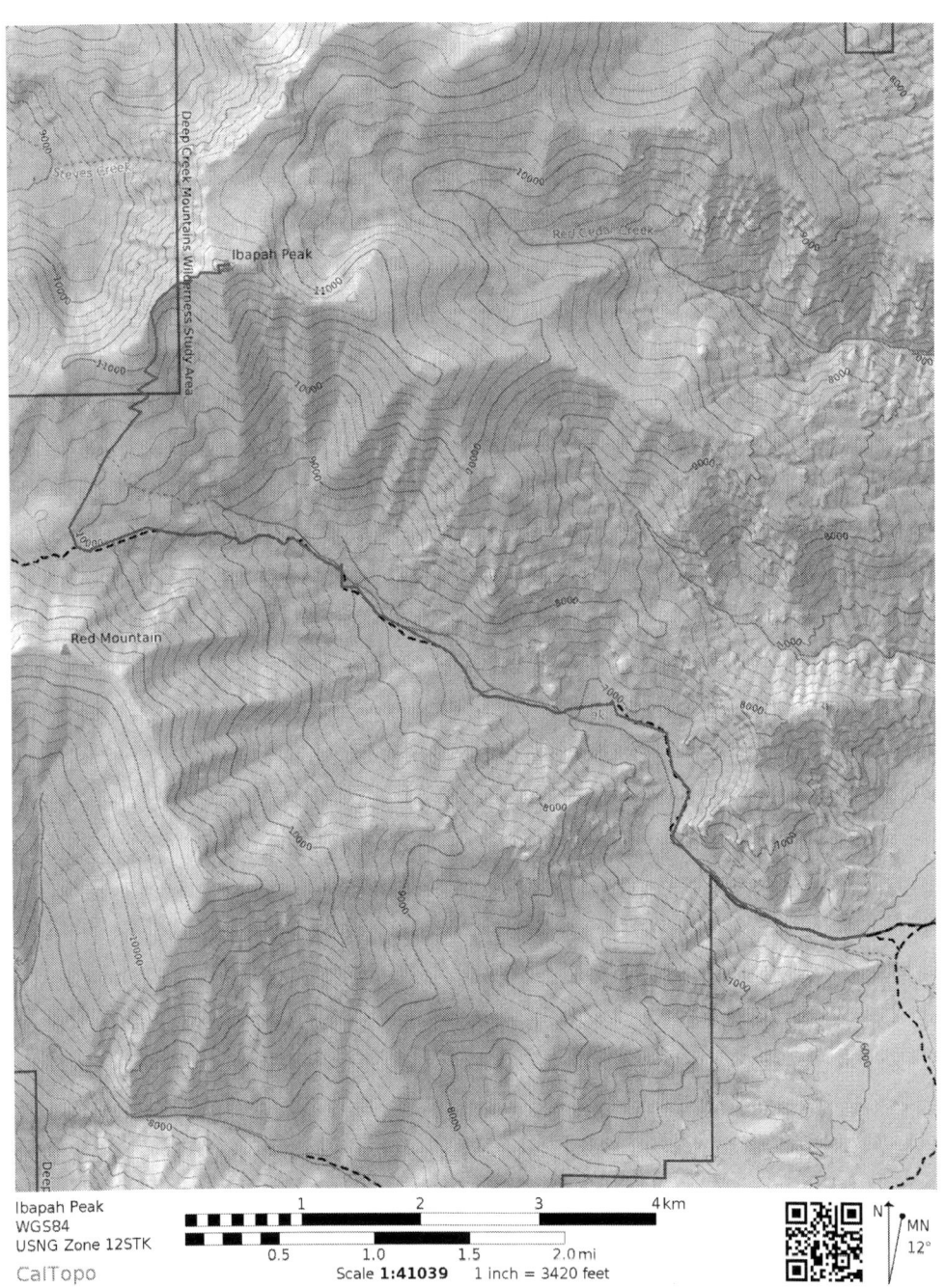

Ibapah Peak
WGS84
USNG Zone 12STK

CalTopo

Scale **1:41039**   1 inch = 3420 feet

Delano Peak, Beaver & Paiute Counties

Stats

Distance: 3.5 miles RT

Elevation gain: 1,612 ft

Time: 2-4 hours

Dog friendly? Yes, off-leash

Kid friendly? No, due to
    steep/rocky terrain

Fees/Permits? None

Best season? Late summer
    and fall

Comment

Delano Peak (12, 169 ft) is the county high point for both Beaver & Paiute Counties and sits to the east of Beaver, UT in the Tushar Mountains. The Tushars have three peaks over 12K Ft - Delano, Mt. Belknap, and Mt. Baldy. The hike to the summit is short and steep, yet very rewarding. The views from the summit can't be beaten! The trail is very exposed — no shade or water is available, so make sure to bring at least 2 liters of water.

Getting There

Drive south on I-15 and take exit 112 in Beaver, UT. Turn left, and drive on Main St. for 1.6 miles. Turn left for UT-153, and drive 16.3 miles. Just past mile marker 16, look for the dirt road turning off to the Northside of the road and turn here. Reset your odometer. The road is a well-graded, dirt road. 4x4 cars are recommended, but a small, compact car can make it only if the road is totally dry. Call the Beaver Ranger station before heading out to check road conditions & to make sure the winter gate is open at 435.896.9233.

0.3 miles — stay left at the first road split

0.8 miles — pass the metal gate

2.4 miles — keep left

3.3 miles - Pass the Paiute ATV Trail, and the road curves right, pass Big John Flat, pass the first pit toilet, and cross a cattle guard

4.3 miles - pass a 2nd pit toilet

4.7 miles - pass the Skyline Recreation TH and a yurt

5.0 miles - drive past Griffith Creek (it may be scorched in Summer/Winter)

5.5 miles - TH will be on the right, with a small brown post/sign. Park here.

Total drive time from SLC is about 3.5-4 hours.

The Route

The trailhead has parking for 2-3 cars. The only sign that marks the trail is a brown post with a yellow sticker and no motorized traffic sign. Within 5 minutes, you'll see a sign for FR224 (as this used to be an old jeep road). Continue following the jeep road along the ridge. Eventually, it will turn into a single-track trail. Pass by several tall, old wooden fence posts. Only a few cairns mark the way. Aim for the false summit, and you notice the trail dies out for a little bit. You'll reach the saddle, then can clearly see your destination from here. Continue to the summit, which is marked by a large green sign with the name and elevation.

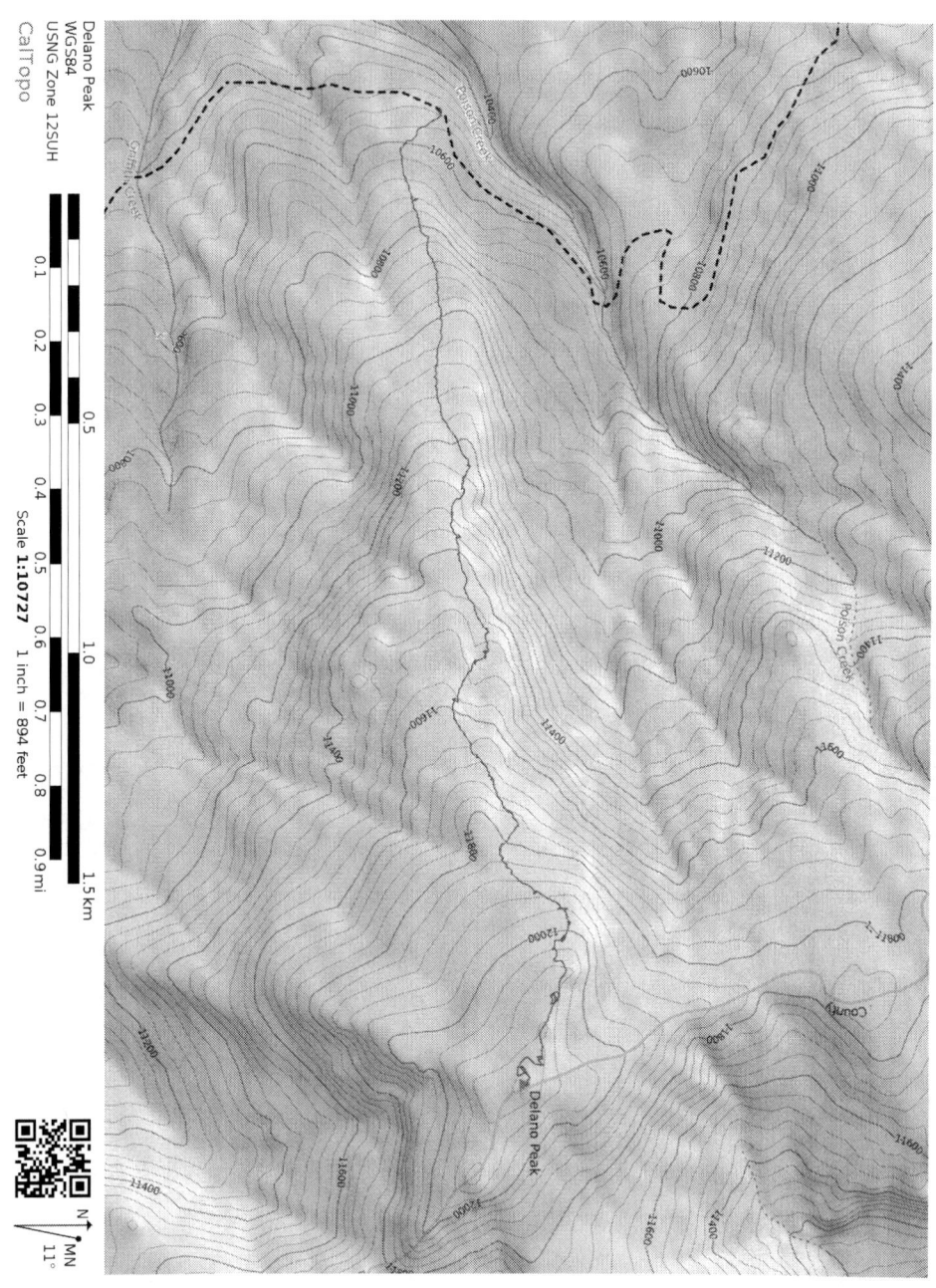

Eccentric Benchmark, Uintah County & Dagget County

Stats

Distance:

To summit is 3 miles one way

To do the whole loop is 10 miles RT

Elevation gain: 1,667 ft

Time: 2 hours to summit, 5-7 hours for full loop

Dog friendly? Yes, off-leash. Dogs should be used to hiking over lots of rocks and boulders.

Kid friendly? Yes, depends on peak-bagging experience

Fees/Permits? None

Best season? Lake summer and Fall

Comment

Eccentric Benchmark (12,276 Ft) is the highest point for both Uintah & Daggest Counties in Utah, making it a popular summit for peak baggers. It's a high, rounded mountain in the Far East Uintas. What it lacks in views from the summit makes up along the cross country trek with views as far as King's Peak to the West and the Flaming Gorge to the Northeast. Although there is no official trail leading to the summit, hiking here is actually quite easy. You'll first pass by three man-made lakes (Chepeta, Papoose, & Moccasin), then work up a short but steep boulder field before hiking across high-alpine terrain and reaching the peak.

You'll want to start hiking early, though, as the Uintas regularly get afternoon thunderstorms. Always carry a rain jacket and mosquito repellent in the Uintas, and for this hike, you'll need at least 2 liters of water (more if you bring dogs).

If you are short on time and only want to bag Eccentric Benchmark, do that. However, if you have a full day to explore, I highly recommend turning this into one big loop. Start by summiting the peak, then walk west along the ridge over to Walk Up Lake, then back down to the car. This will make your trek roughly 10 miles RT and provide several excellent views of the North's drainages, including Sprit, Tamarack, & Dagget Lakes.

Getting There

From SLC, head east on I-80, then south on HWY 40 until you reach Roosevelt, UT. Turn left on HWY 191, then right on HWY 121, heading towards Neola, UT. Veer right on Uintah Canyon Road, and cross the bridge. As soon as you cross the bridge, you'll see the dirt road split right and cross a cattle guard. Reset your odometer to 0. Drive 22 miles along the now, well-graded dirt road following the Elkhorn Canyon Road (Road 117). This road eventually turns into Road 110. Drive to the very end of the road, where the trail begins. The Chepeta Lake TH is where the Highline Trail begins; however, you will want to start hiking from the Chepeta Dam. If you type "Chepeta Dam" into your phone map app, this route should pop up. Otherwise, use my map below. The 22-mile dirt road is mostly well-graded except for a few potholes. Small cars should be able to make it slowly, but a better option would be an SUV or larger. Even though it's only 22 miles, it will take about 45 minutes to reach Chepeta Lake. This road access is only open July - October, or when the road is dry and clear of snow/mud.

The Route

The trail for this route starts at the dam. There's enough parking for 6-7 cars and there is a restroom. Pass by Chepeta Lake. The trail for the first 0.8 miles is very flat and easy walking. Reach Moccasin Lake at 1/2 mile. Past Moccasin Lake veer right at the trail split for Papoose Lake. If you end up doing the loop I describe, you will come back to this  same spot later, coming in from the Wigwam Lake area. At 0.8 miles at Papoose Lake, cross the dam on the East side (to your right). The steepest part is walking up the boulder field right after you cross the dam. It only lasts for 100-200 feet though. After the boulder field, its easy hiking for the next mile, across open high-alpine terrain. Now in the second boulder field, you'll be rock hopping more in between grassy sections. It's a little steeper than before, but not by much. The summit is marked by a large cairn that creates a wall for wind-protection.

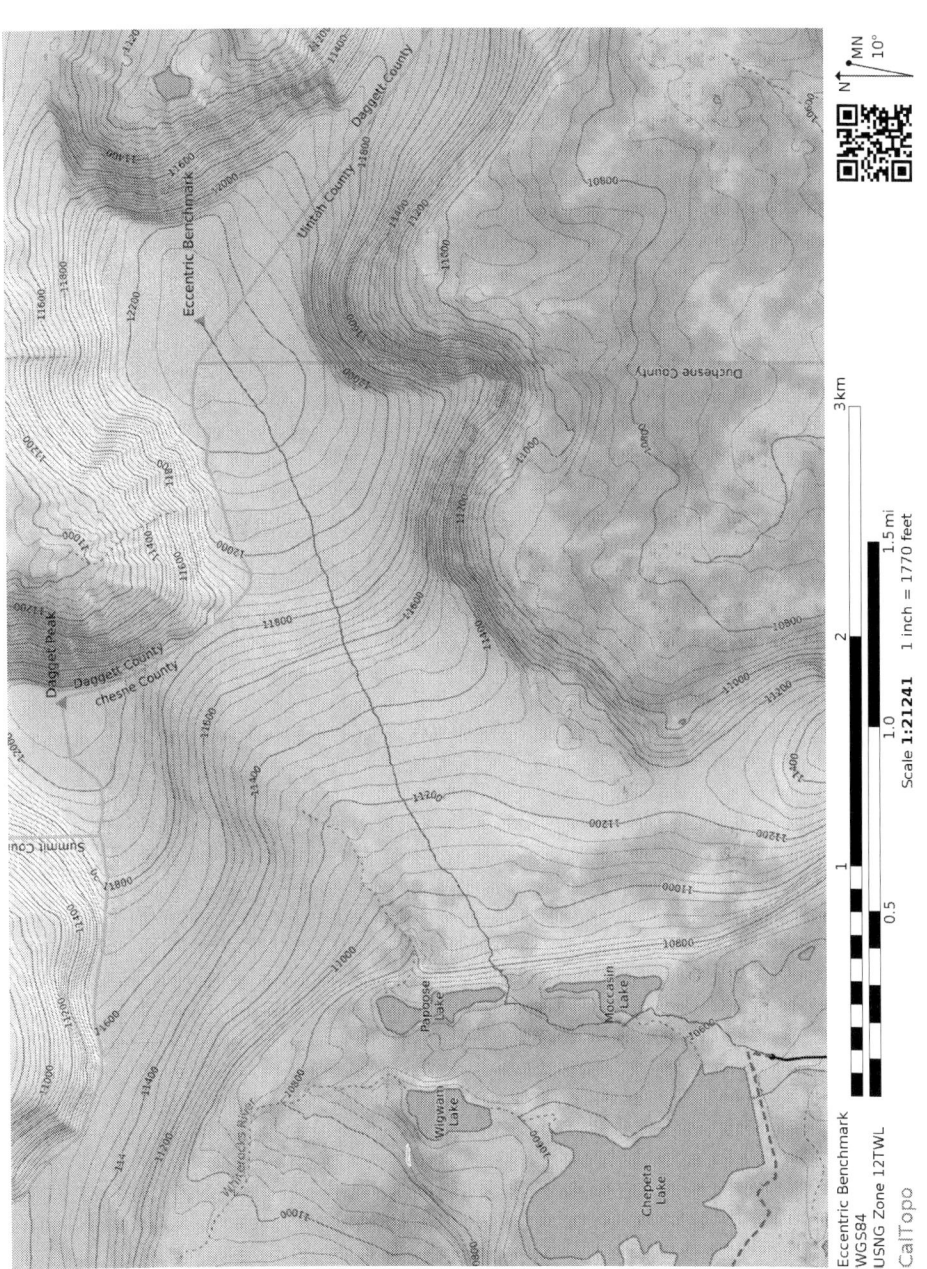

Eccentric Benchmark
WGS84
USNG Zone 12TWL

CalTopo

Scale 1:21241   1 inch = 1770 feet

Mt.Waas, Grand County

Stats

Distance: 8 miles RT

Elevation gain: 2,700 ft

Time: 4-8 hours

Dog friendly? Yes, off-leash

Kid friendly? Maybe for older kids — depends
on their peak bagging experience

Fees/Permits? None

Best Season? Late Summer & fall

Comment

Mt. Waas (12,331 Ft) is the Grand County High Point and the highest peak on the North end of the La Sal Mountains near Moab, Utah. The La Sals can be seen as far away from Green River and parts of Colorado, yet hardly anyone makes the trek to the several summits available, making a great place to seek solitude. The Moab Valley can be in the 100s for daily high temperatures in the summer, yet in the LaSals, it can be at least 20-30F cooler depending on how high you reach. The La Sals area only accessible during summer months when the gates are open and the roads are dry and clear of snow, typically July - October.

One of the best things about the La Sals is that it is a super dog-friendly mountain range. There are no leash laws, and because of all the snowmelt, there are plenty of streams and lakes to visit. Keep in mind that there is obviously wildlife here, and a leash should be handy at all times. Dogs should be able to hike long distances over rocky terrain when summiting any peak in the La Sals. Be prepared with at least 3 liters of water per person/dog.

Getting There

From Moab, UT head East on HWY 128.for 15.5 miles. Turn right at the signed LaSal Scenic Loop Road. Drive 10.7 miles and you will see another LaSal Scenic Loop sign, turn right again. In 4. 7 miles, look for a brown sign for Miners Basin; turn left here. Once you turn, you will see a "road narrows" sign and will now need a 4x4 drive. Drive to the very end of the road, which ends at a dead end and at TH sign.

The Route

Turn at the signed Miner's Basin TH (it is not signed if coming from the South - we had to turn around after missing the turn off initially). Take FR 065 - you WILL need a 4x4 car to reach the TH. I would not advise that even mini-SUVs drive this. Only trucks and a 4Runner were driving along this road. There are also very few pull-

outs — so cross your fingers no one is coming the opposite way! The car more downhill is the one that needs to move — the upper car has the right of way.

For the bulk of the hike, you are hiking on an old jeep/mining road. At the first trail split, go right. You'll quickly cross a stream. Pass a red gate within 15 minutes of hiking. About another 10 minutes past this gate (0.8 miles from the TH), you'll see a junction with no trail split signs — go left. Make sure you are following another old jeep road and hiking uphill. You should be hiking east and now steadily gaining elevation. At 1.4 miles, you'll reach your first switchback. From here, the next 1.5 miles are switchbacks all the way up to the ridge that you can see here. At 3.0 miles, you'll finally reach the saddle and have your first view of Mt. Waas! It looks really far away and super steep, but from the saddle, it's only about 0.8 miles and a net elevation gain of 350 Ft. From the saddle, continue left. Pass the old weather station. The basin below to the East is called Beaver Basin. You can also access Mt. Waas from this side, and drive up pretty close; however, there is no trail. You would just need to pick your own route to the saddle and then catch the trail to the summit. Once again, it doesn't really look like there is a trail, but once you are on it, you can't get lost on the way up. Follow the tight, steep switchbacks up to the summit.

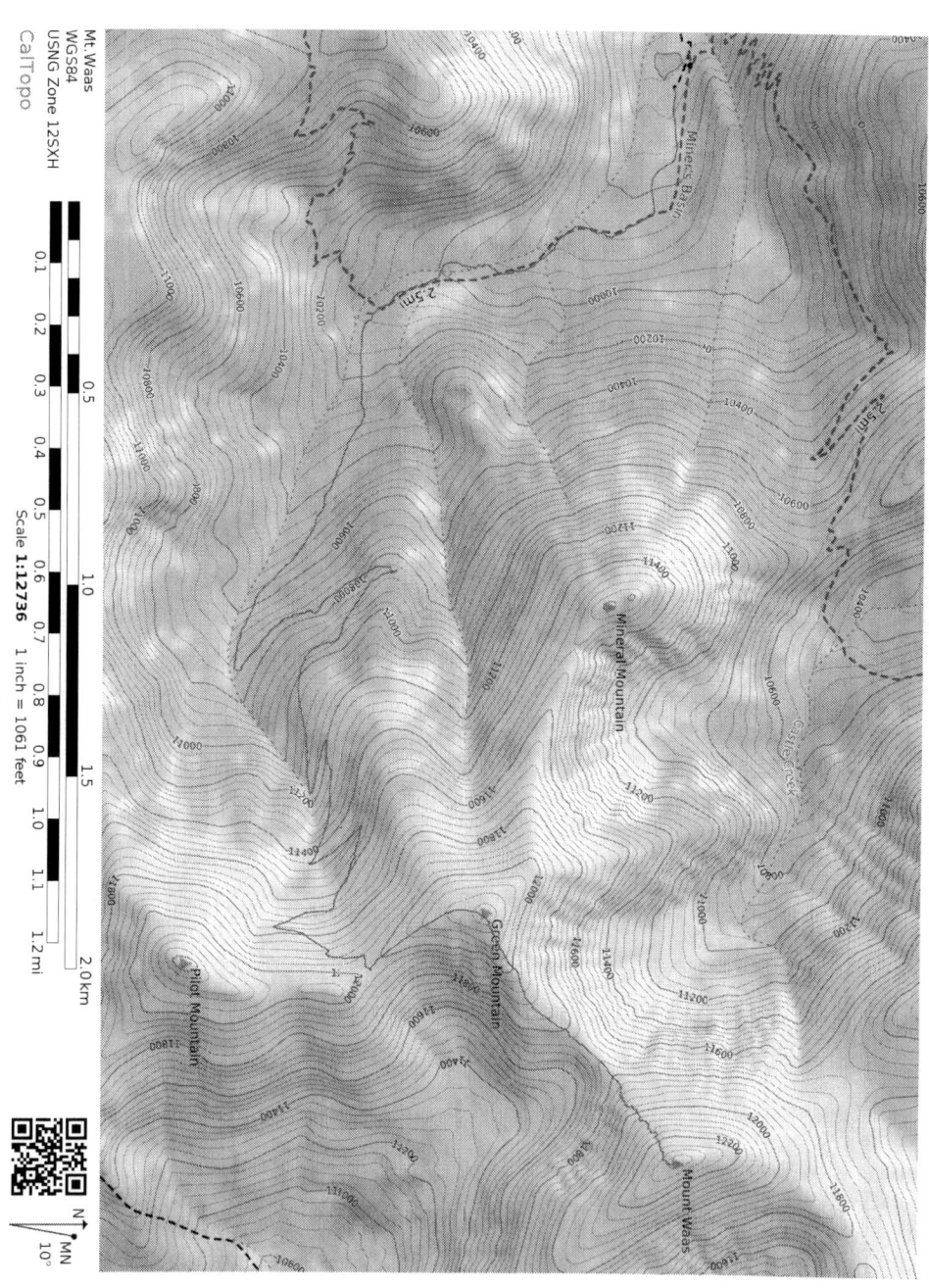

Mt.Peale, Grand County

Stats

This is based on summiting both
Mt. Peale and Mt. Tuk.

Distance: 6.3 miles RT

Elevation gain: 3,400 ft

Time: 6-8 hours

Dog friendly? While Charlie was able
to complete the hike and dogs are
allowed off-leash, I don't
recommend dogs for this trail.

Kid friendly? No

Fees/Permits? None

Best season? Summer or Fall, combined with Mt.Waas on a separate day

Comment

Mt. Peale (12,721 Ft) and Mt. Tukuhnikivatz (12, 482 Ft) are two prominent peaks in the LaSal Mountains right outside of Moab, UT. Mt. Peale is the highest point in the range, and 2nd tallest prominent mountain in Utah; Mt. Tukuhnikivatz (pronounced tuk-oon-ik-ah-vatz) is the peak you mainly see from the valley floor from Moab and is a mountain well known in Edward Abbey's book, *Desert Solitaire*. Hiking to Mt. Peale and Mt. Tukuhnikivatz is not for the average hiker — it requires hiking off-trail, a little route finding, gaining a lot of elevation in a short distance, and requires crossing over the infamous Razor Fang (aka knife edge). The Razor Fang is about a 300 Ft long section of crumbling rock pinnacles and narrow class 3 ridgeline rock climbing. Most people (including me) say this is the most difficult part about the entire hike. While Charlie was able to cross this section, he needed a lot of help, and I don't recommend taking your dog over this. Because the Razor Fang contains loose, crumbling rock and you can't really escape once you are in the midst of it, it is rated as one of Utah's hardest ridge lines. Only very experienced hikers with prior knife-edge exposure should attempt this section. As a comparison, if you've hiked the American Fork Twin Peaks knife-edge in the Wasatch, it's about three times worse than that.

Getting There

The best and easiest way to get to LaSal Pass is by heading south from Moab, UT, on HWY 191 for about 22 miles. Turn left onto HWY 46, and drive another 13.7 miles. Turn left onto HWY 154, and then another left onto HWY 124. This road will curve around to the right, then cross a fairly big stream. Turn left at the sign for LaSal Pass (FR 0073). Stay on this road for another 7-8 miles until you see the sign for Medicine and Beaver Lakes. At this point, if you are camping, you'll want to find a spot somewhere in this area for the night. There are plenty of meadows to camp in, or you can camp at the lakes. Stay on the dirt road until you reach LaSal Pass and the official TH. There are no restrooms. You will need a high clearance car to drive on the dirt road. We had a Jeep Cherokee and Jeep Wrangler and both did great. A small car would have issues and not be able to cross the stream.

FYI, do not take the LaSal Scenic Loop Road by Ken's Lake, then follow the dirt road up and east to the LaSal Pass. We ended up driving down this on our way out, and the road is BAD. It's super rocky, very narrow, steep, and will take 2-3x longer to reach the TH. We were in two Jeeps that could handle this road, but it's more suitable for a Razor, ATV, or dirt bike. Do not take this route!

The Route

Start from the main trail sign, and follow the well-traveled trail up the switchbacks up to the main ridge. Once you reach the ridge, the trail fades away and you are left on your own to find your way to the summit. Part of that is what makes this a fun hike! Work your way up the talus field to Mt. Tuk. While the talus field is  steep and contains loose rock, it's not dangerous. When ready, head back down the ridge towards Mt. Peale. You'll reach a section called the Razor Fang - a very narrow and steep ridge section with loose rock.

This section alone may take you 30-45 minutes because of how slow the hiking is. The trail up to Mt. Peale is easy to follow. Return the way you came, bypassing Mt.Tuk on your way down. Another option is to hike off-trail, bypassing the Razor Fang for a second round, and simply aim downhill. This was our choice, and though it proved to be painful for bad knees, it did shave off quite a bit of mileage and time.

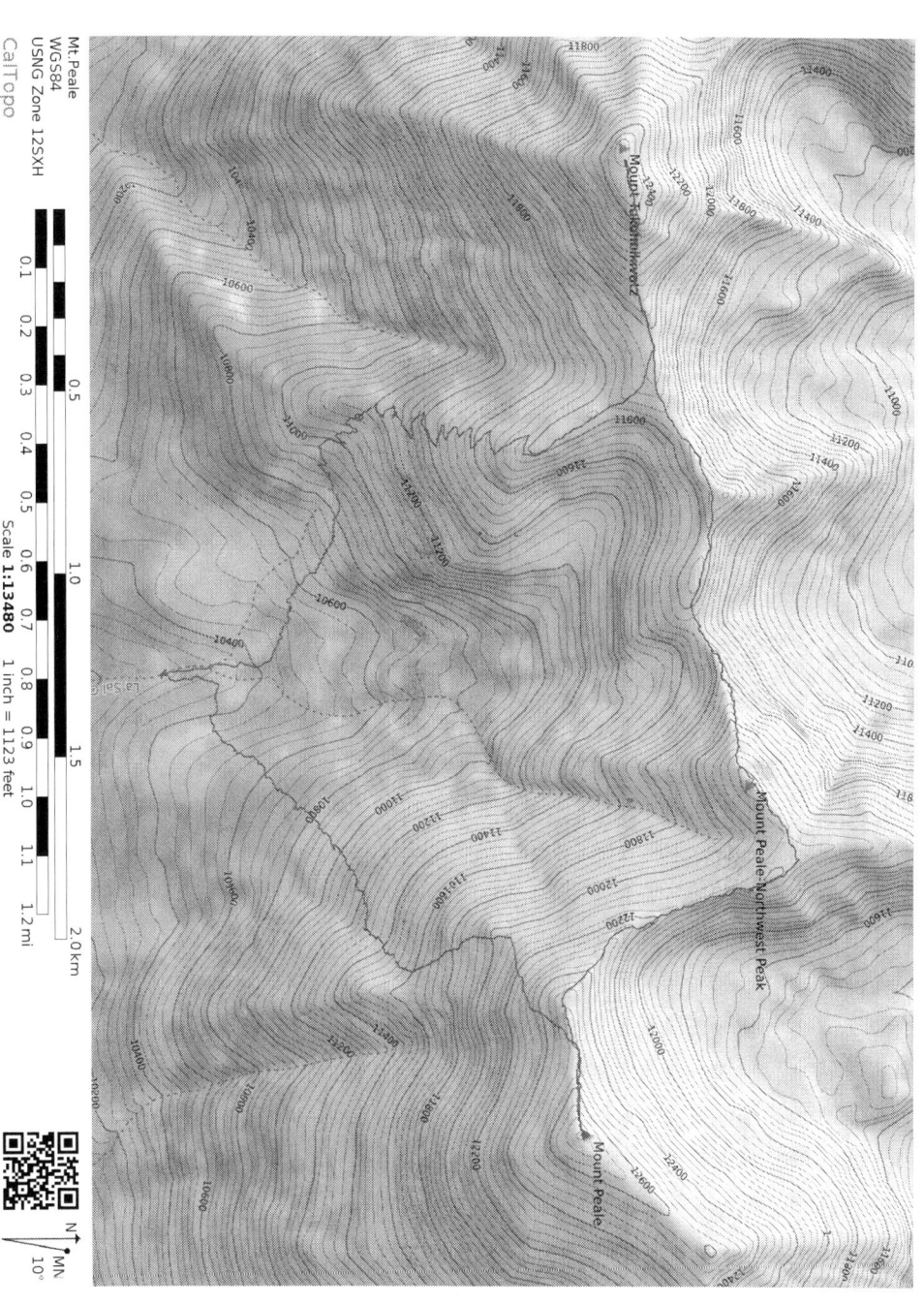

Mt.Peale
WGS84
USNG Zone 12SXH

CalTopo

Scale **1:13480**

1 inch = 1123 feet

Gilbert Peak, Summit County

Stats

Distance:

25 miles RT (total)

9.2 miles to Gilbert Lake

6.3 miles RT (loop) for Gilbert Peak

Elevation gain:

1,840 ft to Gilbert Lake

2,550 Ft from Gilbert Lake to Gilbert Peak

Time:

3-5 hours to Gilbert Lake

5-7 hours for Gilbert Peak (including 1 hour on the summit)

Dog friendly? Yes, off-leash

Kid friendly? Maybe, depends on their backpacking and peak bagging experience

Fees/Permits? None

Best Season? Summer or Fall

Comment

Gilbert Peak (13,442 ft) is the third highest peak in the state and the second-highest county high point. Gilbert Peak can be accessed by several drainages, with Henry's Fork being the most popular; however, I recommend accessing it from Gilbert Lake. The trail to Gilbert Lake follows the West Beaver Creek trail for 9.2 miles before reaching the basin with four  lakes total, great campsites, lots of wildlife, and fairly "easy" access to the peak.

To reach Gilbert Peak you'll need to be comfortable hiking off-trail, route finding, and boulder hoping. It's only 3.5 miles to the summit from Gilbert Lake, yet gains 2,550 ft! Add that to an already high elevation, and it'll leave you short of breath. You'll end up hiking up one of the steep chutes to the ridge, then follow that up and over to the summit. There's nothing technical about climbing this peak, but you should be in decent shape to get there. You can return to the lake the same way or create a loop (what we did), hiking down the SE ridge. This puts you at only 6.3 miles RT. I would highly recommend doing this.

Though Gilbert Peak is very close to its neighbor Kings Peak (the tallest peak in Utah), this peak sees way less traffic and has just as amazing (and even better) views. For county high point peak baggers, this peak is a must.

Dogs that have peak bagging experience, and can hike long distances over rocky and boulder terrain, should do well on this hike. I always carry dog booties for emergencies to scraped up paws. Make sure your dog has at least 1 liter of water minimum. The same goes for kids - as long as they have experience with this they should do well.

This area can only be accessed from July-October when the road is open, the snow is gone, and the trail is dry. Thunderstorms typically happen every afternoon, so be prepared for any kind of weather. On our trip, we got rained on, yet could see snow flying!

Getting There

From the town of Mountain View, WY, head west on 1st Street toward Stadium St. Turn left on WY-410 east. Turn left on Co Rd 283, and continue on FR072. Turn left on FR017, and another left for FR017. Turn right on FR046, then left on FR082. Turn right at the brown sign for West Beaver Creek, and park at the end of the road. I recommend having an SUV or larger to reach the TH. Small cars may have issues with rutted/rocky roads, especially in wet weather.

The Route

The trail is pretty uneventful for the first 3 miles. It follows an old jeep road, and it is on the sandy side. At 2.5 miles, you'll see a small trail sign — keep left. 4.5 miles — reach the High Uintas Wilderness sign. The next trail intersection at 5.7 miles is a little confusing. The map shows to go straight, but you actually have to turn left and cross the river, then it goes straight (south). Somebody has carved "Gilbert" pointing left, and they are correct. About 25 feet from the trail split, you'll cross the West Beaver Creek. As soon as you cross the creek, you'll see the Gilbert Lake signs. Around 7 miles, you'll have your first good view of Gilbert Peak! Cross the creek one more time on a handmade bridge. There were plenty of campsites to choose from here, and even the upper lakes (ranging from 0.5-1.0 mile further). Reach Gilbert Lake

For Gilbert Peak, start by hiking around the West side of the lake, and aim for the ridge. There is no trail. Hug the cliffs on the right heading up, and pick an area to hike straight up, typically in a small chute or gully. Reach the ridge. It's easy hiking for the next 1/2 mile! Continue hugging the Ridgeline as you continue hiking off-trail to reach the summit. The boulders come and go, but it's fairly easy to cross country hiking. Reach the summit.

On our way down, turn this into a loop and hike down the southeast ridge—still more boulders. As you reach the saddle on the southeast side, aim straight down back to the lakes. The saddle had the easiest section of hiking. A nice relief from boulders! At the saddle, picking your route out. There's really only one option - straight down. We did try to make small switchbacks. After dropping back into the basin, it's enjoyable to explore some of the unnamed lakes. Return to camp.

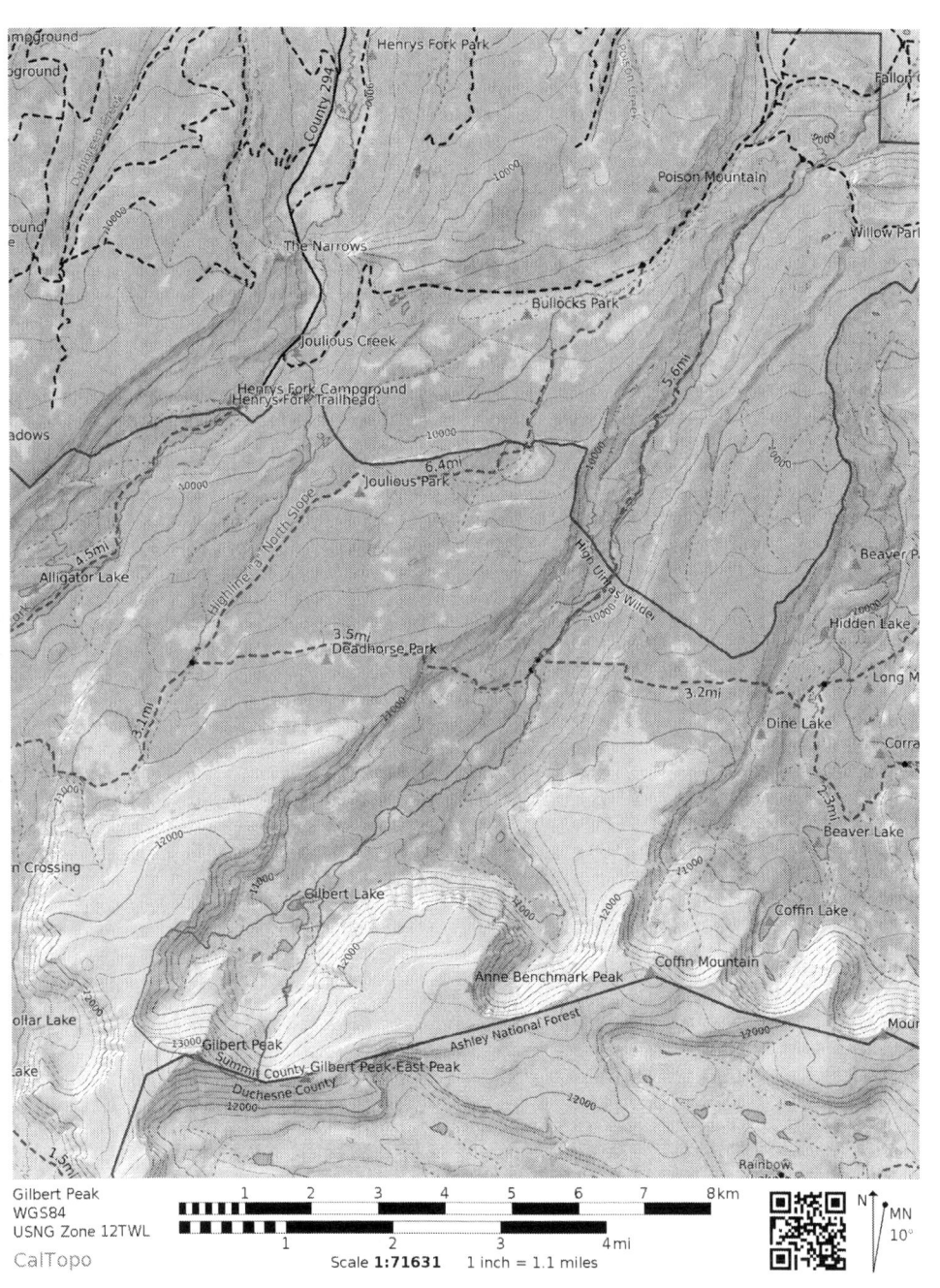

Gilbert Peak
WGS84
USNG Zone 12TWL

CalTopo

Scale **1:71631** 1 inch = 1.1 miles

Kings Peak, Duchesne County

Stats

Distance: 30 miles RT

Elevation gain: 4,100 ft

Time: 6-8 hours for the summit

Dog friendly? Yes, off-leash

Kid friendly? No

Fees/Permits? None

Best season? Summer or Fall

Comment

Kings Peak, located in the Eastern Uinta Mountains, will require a minimum 1-night backpack for most hikers. Some people can do it in one day, but I don't recommend rushing the experience. Getting to the summit is 15 miles one way, and the trail gains roughly 4,100 Ft via the Henry's Fork Trailhead. In 8.4 miles, turn left on Co Rd 283. Continue onto FR072 for 3.7 miles. Turn left onto FR017 in 7 miles. Continue on FR017, following the brown signs for Henry's Fork TH. The total drive time from SLC is roughly 3 hours.

Getting There

Drive east on HWY I-80 through Parley's Canyon and past Evanston, WY. Take exit 34 and turn right, towards Ft.Bridger, WY. Turn right on CoRD 219/Cemetery Rd. Turn left on WY-411 E, then right on WY-410 E.

The Route

From the TH parking area, the trail follows along the West side of Henry's Fork, climbing gently at a grade you will hardly notice. The creek, usually about 20 feet below the trail is clear, and the forest dense. The first lake you'll pass is Alligator Lake, at the end of a short spur trail about 2.3 miles from the TH. You will see the trail branch off to the right of the main trail, and it is 0.4 miles up the drainage. This is the first best option for campsites if you want a shorter day or start hiking late in the day. 5.5 miles from the TH, the trail breaks out of the trees at the end of a meadow, and there is a major trail junction here between Henry's From Trail, which runs south along henry's fork and the North slope trail which crosses in an east-west direction called Elkhorn Crossing. Dollar Lake is the next big attraction, another 2.5 miles away. This is the most popular spot for camping. However, if you want to get away from crowds, keep hiking a little further, but I would suggest staying below the tree line. At 11,888 Ft cross over Gunsight Pass. Continue following the trail as it wraps around the West slope of Painter Basin.

Painter Basin is only 2.9 miles from King's Peak, but you still need to gain 2,100 ft. And a small amount of rock scrambling. Reach Anderson Pass at 12,700 ft. The last 0.8 mile has no trail, as you will be doing some light scrambling over medium-sized boulders. You will gradually see cairns, but hike where it feels comfortable for you and don't rely on them to be available. Make your way to the tallest peak in Utah at 13, 512ft!

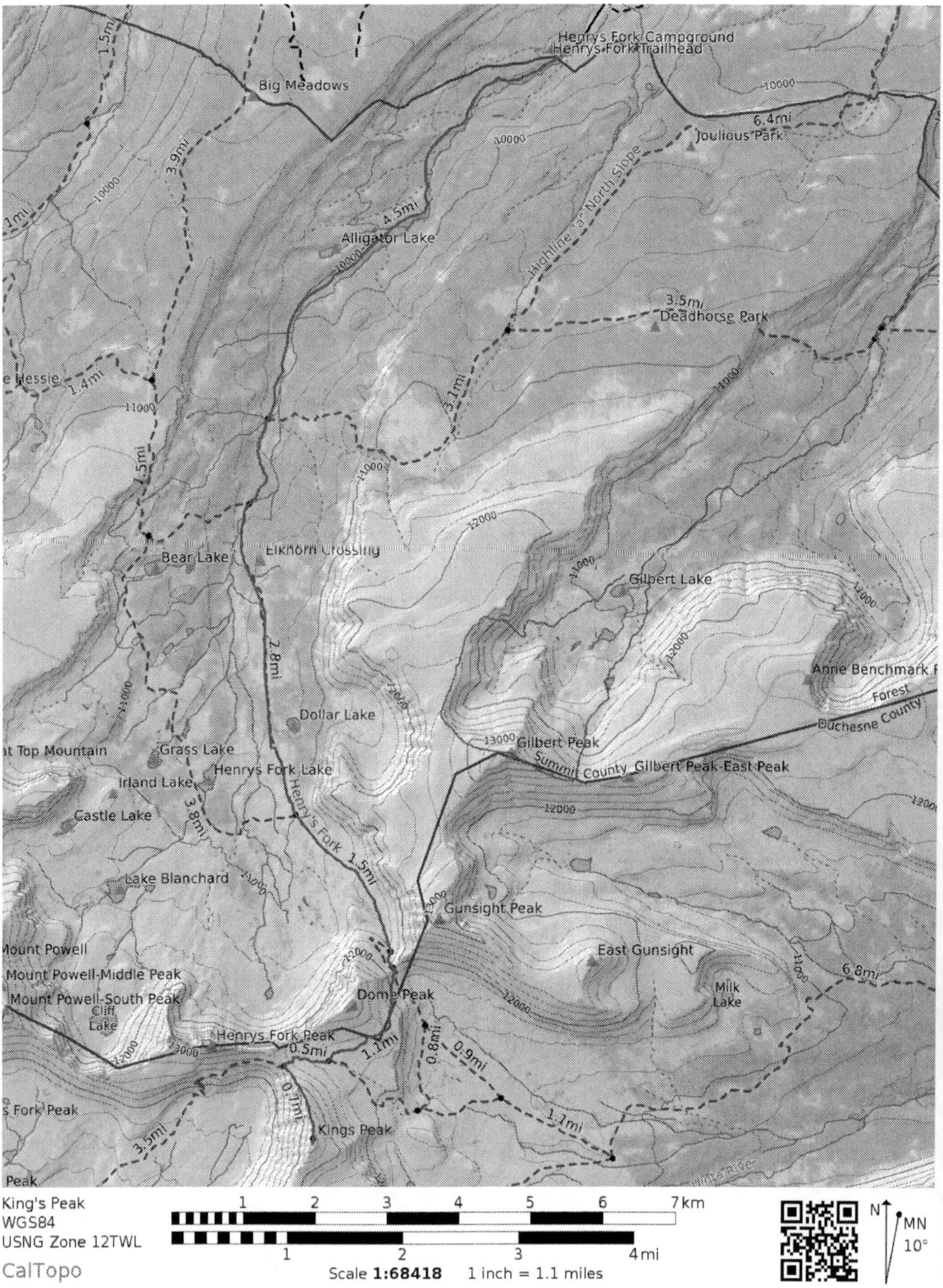

Henrys Fork Campground
Henrys Fork Trailhead
Big Meadows
Joulious Park
Alligator Lake
Highline "a" North Slope
Deadhorse Park
Bear Lake
Elkhorn Crossing
Gilbert Lake
Anne Benchmark
Dollar Lake
Gilbert Peak
Summit County
Gilbert Peak-East Peak
Duchesne County
Forest
Grass Lake
Henrys Fork Lake
Irland Lake
Castle Lake
Henry's Fork
Lake Blanchard
Gunsight Peak
East Gunsight
Mount Powell
Mount Powell-Middle Peak
Mount Powell-South Peak
Cliff Lake
Milk Lake
Dome Peak
Henrys Fork Peak
Kings Peak
King's Peak
WGS84
USNG Zone 12TWL
CalTopo
Scale 1:68418
1 inch = 1.1 miles
MN
10°

Bonus Peaks

Clayton Peak

Stats

Distance: 6 miles RT

Elevation gain: 1800 ft

Time: 2-4 hours

Dog friendly? No, dogs are not
allowed in BCC

Kid friendly? Yes, ages 8+

Fees/Permits? None

Best Season? Summer and Fall

Comment

Clayton Peak (10,721 Ft) is a fun local peak located at Brighton Ski Resort's top in Big Cottonwood Canyon. It's right on the ridge of the watershed, so if hiking this route, dogs are not allowed. Prior to January 2020, dogs could make the summit from Bloods Lake Trailhead, but that has since been illegal due to watershed laws. The photo of the author and Charlie was taken in the summer of 2018. However, this time, my friend and I decided to hike to Clayton Peak via Brighton Ski Resort. I hadn't hiked this route in over four years, so it was time to revisit this trail.

This route is very gradual and makes its way up several long, easy switchbacks until you reach the base of the peak and then climbs steadily up short but steep switchbacks. The views from Clayton Peak are some of the best in the area, in my opinion. On a clear day, you can see as far south as Provo Peak and Hayden Peak to the East. This is a great hike to do after work in the summer months when the days are long and temps are cooler at this elevation.

Getting There

Drive all the way up Big Cottonwood Canyon (BCC) until you reach the end of the road where Brighton Ski Resort is. Park at the main lodge, where there is a giant TH sign and map.

The Route

Start by parking at the giant ski map in front of the lodge. Stay straight on the large, well-worn trail. You'll be on the Lake Mary trail the first 0.8 miles. Hike up a few gradual switchbacks. At 0.8 miles, turn left for Clayton Peak. Hike past Dog Lake and up a small hill through a forested section. Hike below the chairlift and you have the first good view of Clayton Peak ahead. The trail crosses several dirt roads/ski runs. Keep following the trail. Make your way up to the ridge, turn left, and you'll again see Clayton Peak. Follow the dirt road. At 2.3 miles, you'll see a cairn and a trail split off to the right. Take this uphill. The trail narrows and you'll hike up several small but steep switchbacks. Hike up through the boulder field - no scrambling is required on this hike. Reach the summit.

(This photo was taken using a different trail so I could bring Charlie with me)

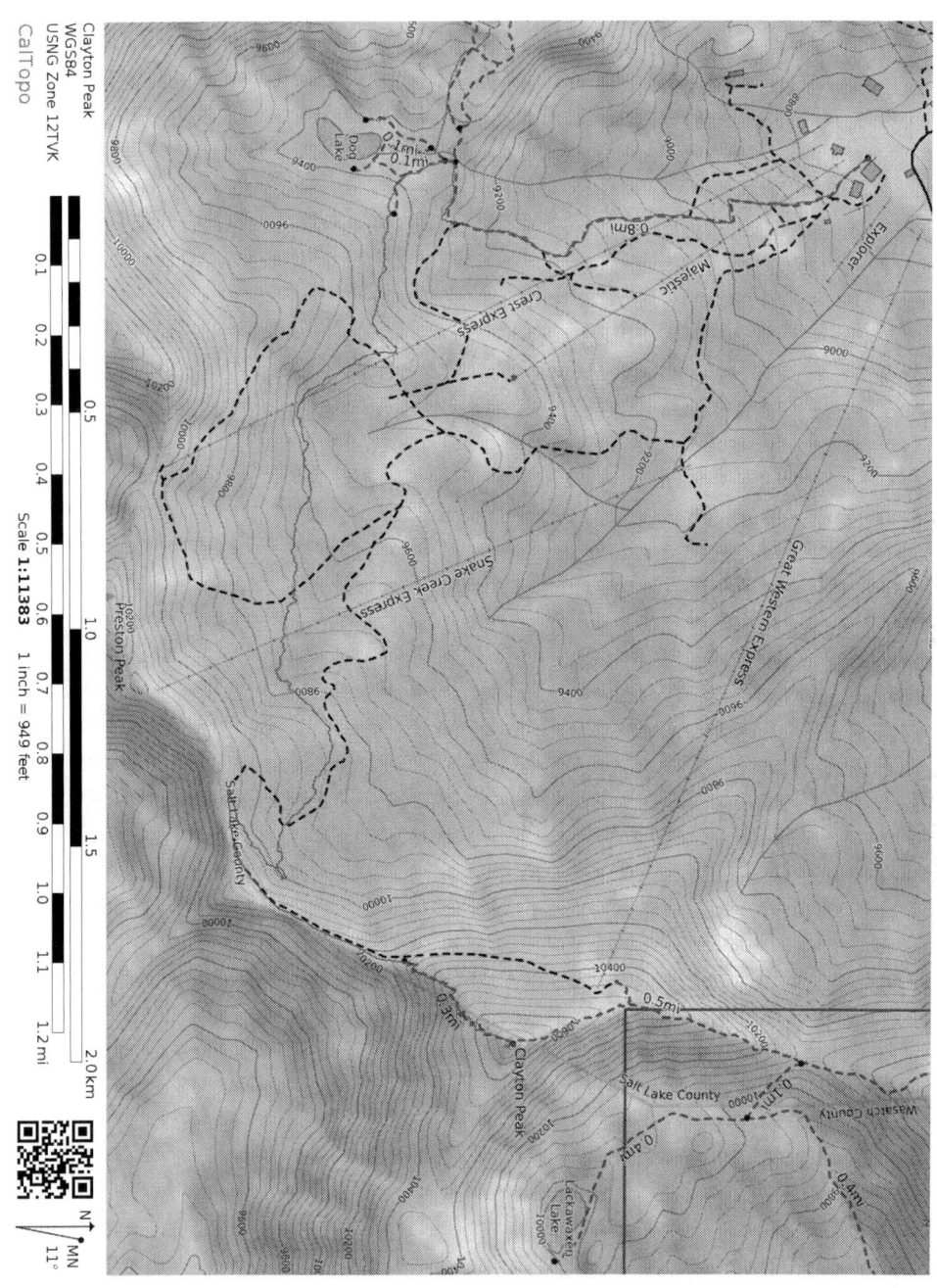

Mt. Ogden

Stats

Distance: 4 miles RT

Elevation gain: 900 ft.

Time: 2-4 hours

Dog friendly? Yes. Technically dogs are to remain on leash on Snowbasin grounds; however, once you are away from people it's fine to have them off-leash as long as they are under control. If your dog is not used to rocky, ridge-type terrain, I don't recommend they hike with you. For some dogs, the rocks may tear up their paws/pads.

Kid friendly? Yes

Best season? Summer & Fall

Fees/Permits: The gondola cost $14 for an all-day pass for adults. Dogs can ride for free. Parking at the Snowbasin lot is free.

Comment

Mount Ogden (9,579 Ft) is home to Snowbasin Ski Resort, where the 2002 Winter Olympic downhill ski races were held. This is a popular summit during the summer when hikers are able to either hike from the base of the mountain or take the gondola up to the Needles Lodge then traverse to the peak.

Getting There

From SLC, drive north on I-15 and take exit 395 towards HWY 89 north, just after the Lagoon. Drive 16 miles, then take I-84 east towards Morgan, UT. Take exit 92 for Snowbasin Ski Resort, and continue following the signs for Snowbasin.

The Route

Once we got off the gondola, veer left, then hike right up to the saddle. Once on the saddle, continue right aiming North. The trail is well-traveled. Reach the summit, marked my cell towers and a helicopter pad.

Mount Ogden

Floyd Iverson Ridge

The Needles

Mt.Ogden
WGS84
USNG Zone 12TVL
CalTopo

0.1   0.2   0.3   0.4   0.5 km

0.1   0.2   0.3 mi
Scale 1:4725   1 inch = 394 feet

N
MN
11°

Frary Peak

Stats

Distance: 7.2 miles RT

Elevation gain: 2,015 ft

Time: 3-4 hours

Dog friendly? Yes, on leash

Kid friendly? No

Fees? $10 entrance fee per car

Comment

Frary Peak (6,578 ft) on Antelope Island State Park is not only the highest point on the island but also the most beautiful trail that offers 360-degree views of the Great Salt Lake, the Wasatch Mountains, and views of the cities. This hike is best to hike between November-March when the horseflies are gone for winter. After March, it is recommended to wear head nets to protect your face against flies. Along this trail, you may see Buffalo, Antelope, and other small animals.

In addition to hiking, Antelope Island is popular for cyclists and runners, and a few races are held on the island. Millions of birds congregate along the shores, offering unparalleled opportunities for bird watching. The Fielding Garr Ranch House (located at the southern end of the island) is an important part of the island and distinctive for two reasons. 1) it is the oldest continually inhabited Anglo home in Utah, and 2) it is the oldest Anglo built house in Utah on its original foundation. Antelope Island is part of what is known as the Basin and Range, stretching from the Wasatch mountains to the east Sierra Nevada mountains to the west. Antelope Island encompasses 28,000 acres, stretching 15 miles long and about 5 miles at its widest.

What's that smell?

The Great Salt Lake supports bacteria whose byproduct is rotten-egg smelling hydrogen sulfide. The worst smell is while crossing the causeway. Once you reach the island, the smell goes away.

Getting There

From SLC, head north on I-15 and take exit 332 for Antelope Drive. Drive across the causeway, and at your first road split, veer left. Turn left again, following the signs for Frary Peak Trail.

The Route

The trail begins steeply, working its way up for about the first mile. You'll notice that the whole island does not have any shade nor water. Be prepared to carry a minimum of 3 L of water per person, and wear and hat and bring sunblock. The trail cuts through a large rock area, with the trail going into it,

then coming out the other side. Once on the ridge, you'll see many dead trees with no shrub on them. They most likely caught on fire years ago or were struck by lighting. Once you reach the weather tower and mile 3, you have two options for reaching the peak. My recommendation is to head right, down the more popular route, and up to the peak. It gets steep in one section, but I prefer hiking up steep trails rather than hiking down steeply. The trail will curve around the south side of the summit. Once you are at the top of the peak, I like to come back along the ridge, hiking in a counterclockwise direction. However, if you are feeling super adventurous, you can hike up and down the ridge. Follow the main trail all the way back down.

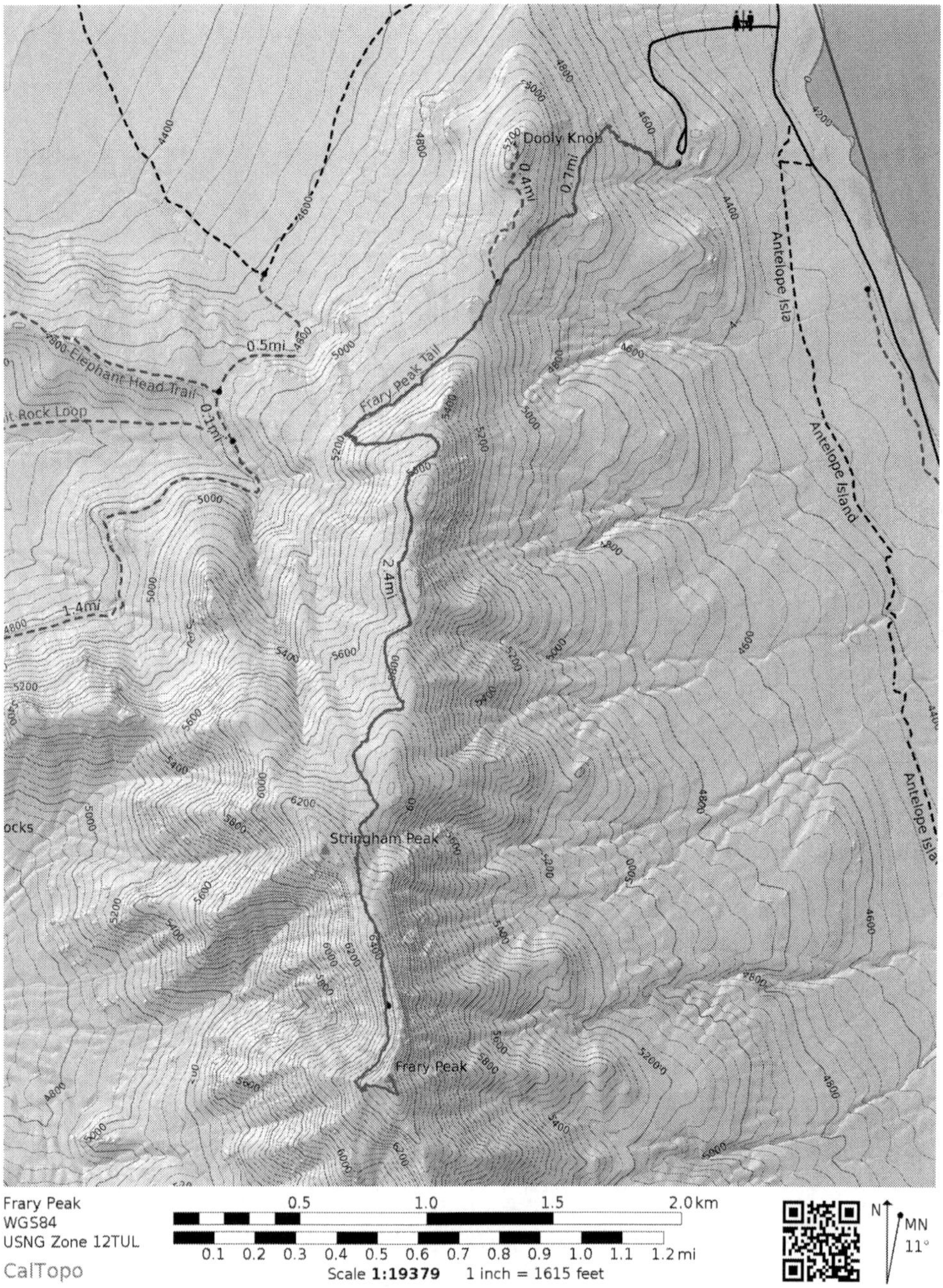
Dooly Knob
0.4mi
0.7mi
Antelope Isla
Antelope Island
0.5mi
Elephant Head Trail
Frary Peak Tail
Rock Loop
0.1mi
2.4mi
1.4mi
Stringham Peak
Frary Peak
Frary Peak
WGS84
USNG Zone 12TUL
CalTopo
0.5 1.0 1.5 2.0 km
0.1 0.2 0.3 0.4 0.5 0.6 0.7 0.8 0.9 1.0 1.1 1.2 mi
Scale 1:19379 1 inch = 1615 feet
N
MN
11°

Bald Mountain (Uintas)

Stats

Distance: 3 miles RT

Elevation gain: 1,100 ft

Time: 2-4 hours

Dog friendly? Yes, off-leash

Kid friendly? Yes

Fees/Permits? There is a $6 fee for a 3-day pass on the Mirror Lake Highway, which you must display in your windshield at all times. It's FREE if you have the annual National Park Pass, American Fork Canyon pass, or Mirror Lake Highway pass. No permit is required to hike Bald Mountain.

Comment

Bald Mountain (11,942 ft) in the High Uintas Wilderness is one of my favorite peaks to summit. Not only is this peak one of the easiest to summit in the area, but it also offers grand views of the Mirror Lake Highway, surrounding lakes, several peaks, and on a clear day, you can see Mt. Timpanogos. Along the Bald Mountain trail, you may see mountain goats, pika, squirrels, and an abundance of wildflowers in early summer. As with any high altitude terrain, start this hike early in the day to beat the daily afternoon thunderstorms, the afternoon heat, and crowds.

This trail contains no obstacle, except for leftover snow that remains well into mid-July depending on snowpack from Winter. This can sometimes frustrate hikes, making them turn back. However, you can easily skirt around it by dropping a little lower, then climbing back up the rocks (keep an eye out for cairns). When snow is not present, hikers of all abilities have a little problem with this route. Keep in mind that when you begin hiking, you are already at 10,500 ft, so some people immediately feel elevation sickness. To prevent this, drink plenty of water, and again, start early to beat the heat. If you feel sick, take your time hiking up to the summit, but of course, listen to your body and if it's saying not to continue, listen to that voice. I've dealt with my fair share of elevation sickness and it's not fun!

Getting There

From SLC drive East on I-80 through Parley's Canyon and past Kimball Junction, UT. Take exit 146 for HWY 40, then take exit 4 towards Kamas, UT. At the first stoplight, turn left. At the next stoplight (at the Chevron), turn right, which will put you on the Mirror Lake Highway. Drive 29 miles until

you reach Bald Mountain Pass, and look for the small dirt road to the left with a sign that says Bald Mountain Picnic area & Trailhead. There is one vault restroom. The parking lot in summer is almost always full. Don't let it make you think the trail is packed - this parking lot serves as the TH for several other lakes and a shuttle lot for backpackers to drop a car on their multiday trips.

The Route

When you start, the trail immediately splits - right for Bald Mountain, left for the other lakes. Work your way up the rocky trail, which starts gaining elevation right away. You will hike up three small switchbacks; then the trail aims straight. At this point, you will still be hiking on the East side of the mountain. The main trail now cuts through low brush, but only for about 5 minutes. There is zero shade and water on this trail. Even at a high elevation, you can get easily sunburned - bring plenty of sunblock, a hat, and a minimum of 2 L of water with you. The trail will wrap around to the east side of the mountain again. You will see what looks like a trail split here, but stay left. Going right just leads to an overlook. As you get up higher in elevation, you will notice that it gets pretty windy. Even in summer, I bring a long sleeve shirt with me on this hike - you never know how cold it can be at the summit from the wind. Reach the summit.

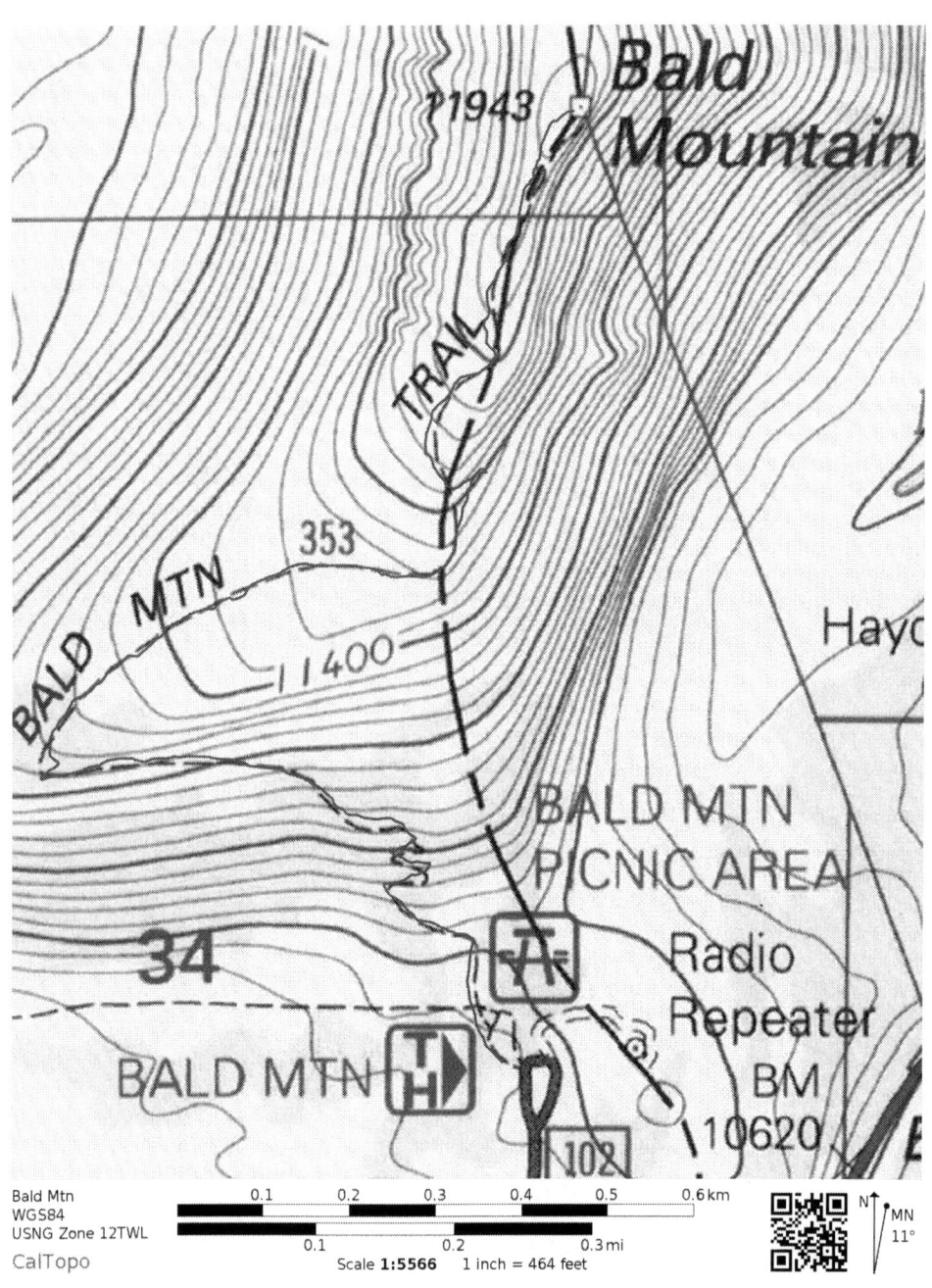

Bald Mtn
WGS84
USNG Zone 12TWL
CalTopo

Scale **1:5566**   1 inch = 464 feet

MN
11°

Reids Peak (Uintas)

Stats

Distance: 2.5 miles one way to Reids Peak

Elevation gain: 1,157 ft

Time: 2-3 hours to summit Reids Peak

Dog friendly? Yes, off-leash.

Kid friendly? No

Fees/Permits? The Mirror Lake Highway charges a $6 fee for a 3-day pass. It's free if you have an annual Mirror Lake Hwy or American Fork Canyon pass, or free if you have an annual National Park Pass. No permit is required.

Comment

Reids Peak (11,708 ft) is located in the High Uintas Wilderness, just off the Mirror Lake Highway. While its neighbor peak, Bald Mountain, see hundreds of hikers each summer, less than 50 people will make the Reids Peak summit each year, and for good reason. There is no trail to the summit and it requires light scrambling, so it's not a good peak for the average/newbie hiker. Typically, only experienced peak baggers are the ones looking to make the summit, and knowledge of route finding will make this hike successful.

With that being said, there is nothing technical about this hike. I never felt unsafe while doing this as a solo hike, and the route I chose seemed to be a path for others when I found several cairns leading to the top. The scrambling itself isn't hard - it's the steepness that makes it more difficult. You're already hiking at a high elevation (11k), so to climb up closet to another 800 ft will slow you down. If you have any scrambling and off-trail experience, you will do fine on this summit.

Dogs are also allowed on this route but be advised that not all dogs do well in this type of terrain. They should be used to hiking over boulders, steep routes, and be ok with the occasional assist from you if needed. I had to boost Charlie up about 2-3 times, but he was able to do everything himself on the way down. Ultimately he could have found a different way up himself, but I wanted him to stick close by me since I was unfamiliar with this route and didn't want him to get hurt without me being able to see him. I would only bring kids up here if they too have a peak experience. Once on the saddle. Continue to the left and up the ridge. You'll want to stay close to the ridge, but not actually *on* it. The rocks are loose in spots, so staying left of it is safer.

Getting There

From SLC drive East on I-80 through Parley's Canyon and past Kimball Junction, UT. Take exit 146 for HWY 40, then take exit 4 towards Kamas, UT. At the first stoplight, turn left. At the next stoplight (at the Chevron), turn right, which will put you on the Mirror Lake Highway. Drive 29 miles until you reach Bald Mountain Pass, and look for the small dirt road to the left with a sign that says Bald Mountain Picnic area & Trailhead. There is one vault restroom.

The Route

The Bald Mountain trailhead gets packed quickly, so it's wise to start early not only to beat the heat but also find parking. Turn left at the very first sign. Going right takes you to Bald Mountain, and if you do the loop I did, you'll end up coming down from this side. You'll cross four bridges and will be hiking downhill. Between 0.8-1.0 miles is where you'll want to turn off to the right. Anywhere in between that works to start aiming towards the Reids Peak saddle. You just want to make sure you stay out of the boulder field on the west side of Bald Mountain. Aim for the saddle - for me, getting up to the saddle was harder than the actual ridge to the peak. It was super steep with loose rock, and I kept running into the low evergreen bushes. A few times, I had to turn around, then find a better way up. The "trail" is the typical Uinta boulders you can just step up and over. There were maybe 2-3 sections that Charlie needed a boost on but otherwise could do it independently. Work steeply up a very faint trail to the summit.

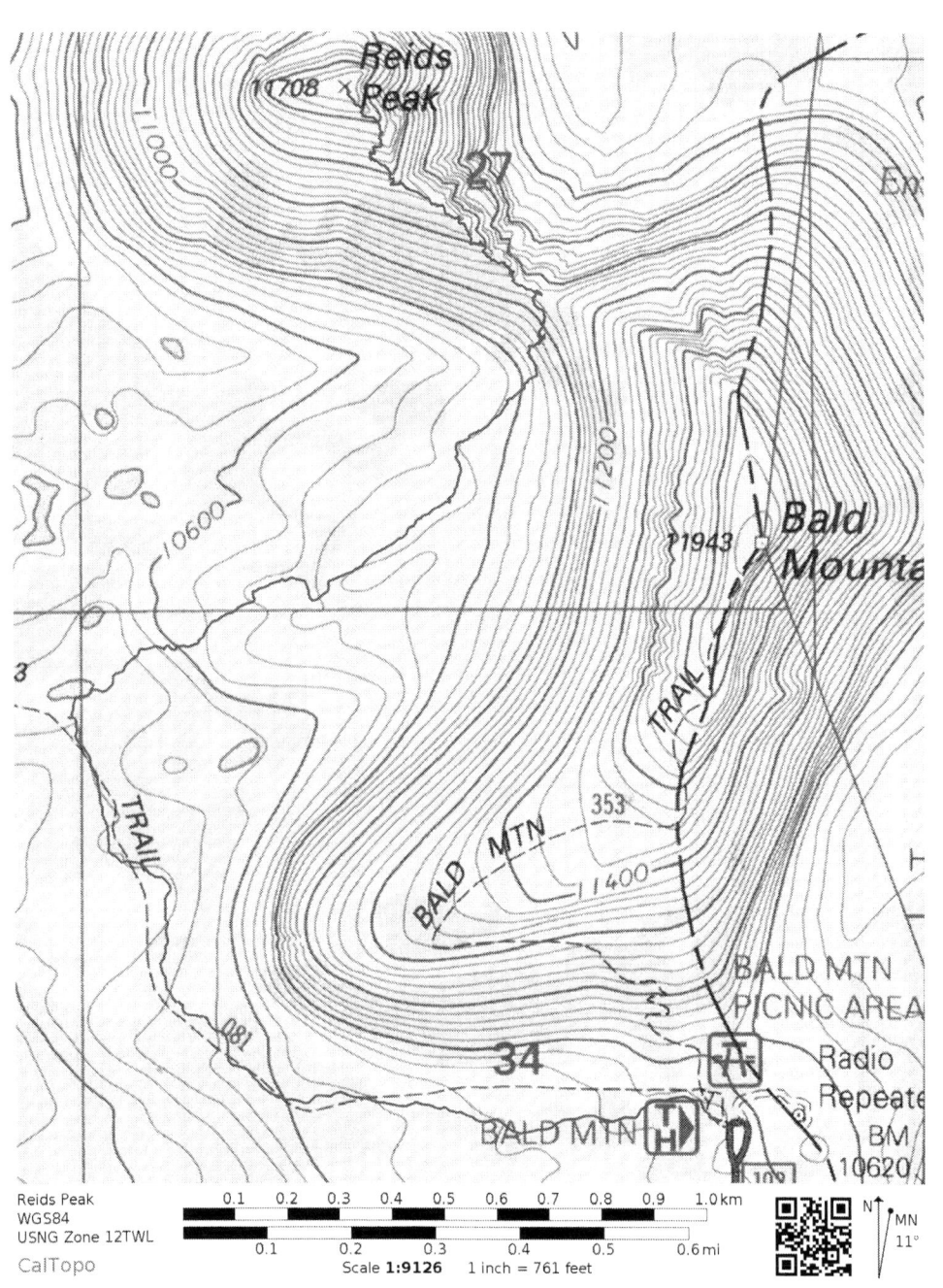

Reids Peak
WGS84
USNG Zone 12TWL

CalTopo

Scale **1:9126**   1 inch = 761 feet

Mt.Superior & Monte Cristo

Stats

Distance: 5.2 mi RT

Elevation gain: 2,500 ft

Time: 3-5 hours

Dog friendly? No, dogs aren't
    allowed in LCC

Kid friendly? No

Fees/Permits? None

Best season? Summer and Fall

Comment

Mount Superior (11,040ft) & Monte Cristo Peak (11,132 Ft) are two classic and iconic Wasatch Peaks that every peak bagger should summit. Both peaks dominate the Little Cottonwood Canyon Ridge and are focal points to the North when skiing at Alta or Snowbird. Both Mt. Superior and Monte Cristo are summited year-round — in the winter by backcountry skiers and in the summer by hikers looking for a fun little scramble.

The trail has several switchbacks, steadily gaining elevation. Many people hike to Cardiff Pass and turn around, but the real fun and adventure begin when you start to hike along the ridge. The first 1/2 mile of the ridge is easy, and follows a well-defined trail. The last 1/2 mile to the summit is a scramble, with a little route finding. As long as you stay on the ridge, you'll reach the peak. If you are afraid of heights or have never hiked across a knife-edge, this isn't the hike for you. The narrowest section of the ridge is only 1 ft wide!

On this trail, you'll summit Mt. Superior first, and Monte Cristo Peak is a mere 15 minutes further West along the ridge. In my opinion, the ridge in between the two peaks is easier than the climb up to Mt. Superior. Be sure to bag both peaks - it's well worth the effort and time. Start hiking early in the morning in the summer to beat the heat and crowds.

Getting There

Drive up Little Cottonwood Canyon for 8 miles (past the Park in Ride, at the intersection), and park at the "Our Lady of the Snows Center" on your left.

The Route

The trail starts by walking up the paved road right by the Our Lady of the Snows Center and take the first right. You'll then walk by the Sheriff's Station on your left as the road rounds the corner. The road will turn West and turn into a dirt road. The dirt road turns East again. You'll follow the power lines most of the hike until you reach Cardiff Pass. Just after the road turns East, look for the trail splitting off to the left. This is your trail. It's an old mining road that turns into a hiking trail. You'll come to a distinct trail split. To get to Cardiff Pass, go left. Hike through the small meadow, and follow the trail until you reach the pass. Once at Cardiff Pass, turn left (West) and follow the covered electrical line up a rocky area. Bypass Christmas Tree Peak on the left. The trail is well defined along this section of the ridge up to Mt. Superior. Now you can see the trail gets really steep and there's more rocks. Starting here, be very careful where you step and keep an eye out for cairns hikers have placed. The higher you stay on the trail, the closer to the ridgeline you'll be. If you drop down, it's much harder to climb back up and you'll get yourself into loose gravel. A few sections require some easy climbing up to the ridge. Give your friends below some room, in case you accidentally kick rocks down to them. Another tip — keep everything in your pack, not your pockets. Phones, cameras, etc can easily fall out. Summit Mt. Superior. While you are on the ridge, you might as well hike another 15 minutes to bag Monte Cristo Peak! It looks much further and more intimidating than it really is. This section of the ridge was easier than the climb up to Mt. Superior. Return the way you came.

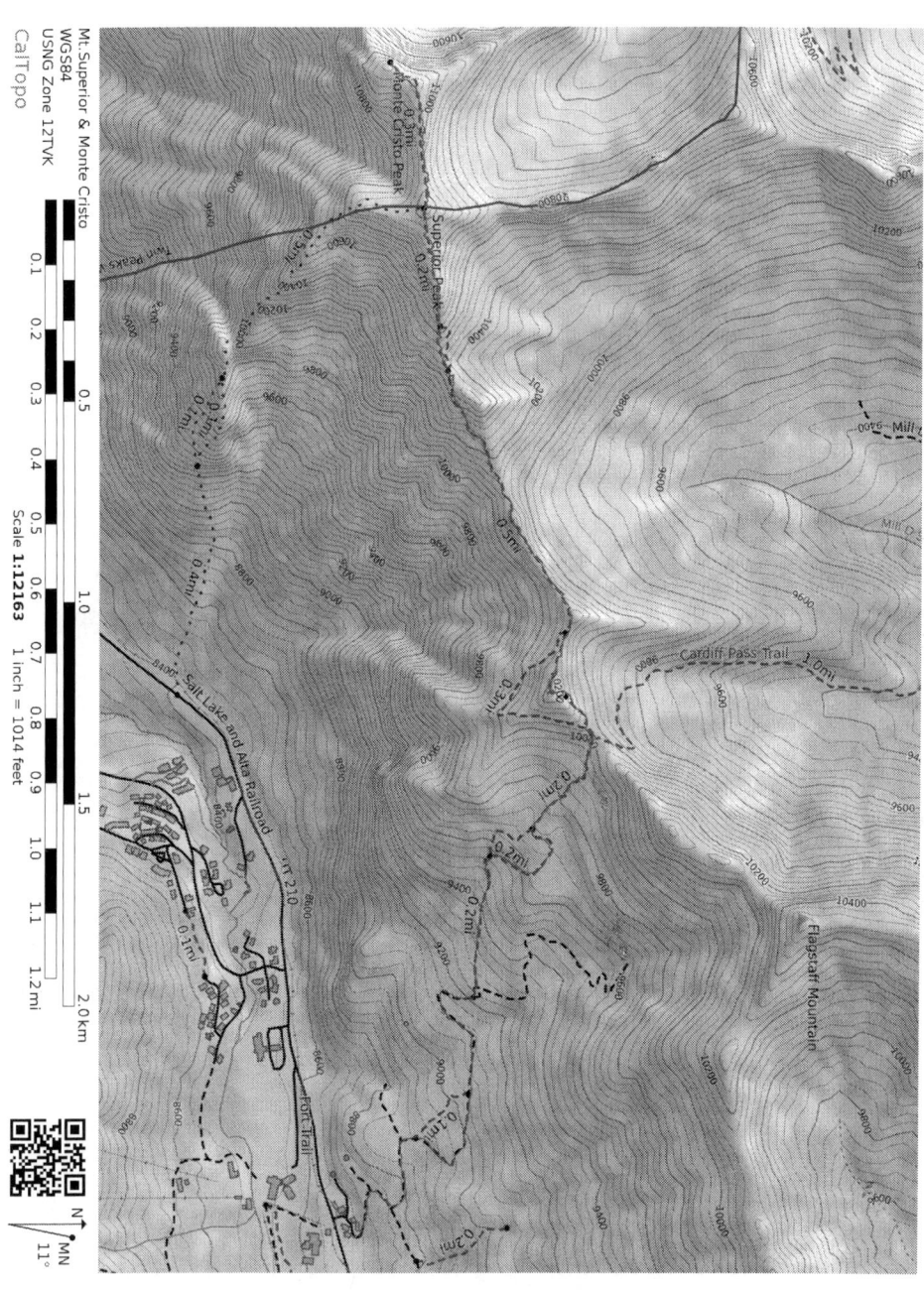

Lewis Peak

Stats

Distance: 10.4 miles RT

Elevation gain: 2,400 ft

Time: 4-6 hours

Dog friendly? Yes, off-leash

Kid friendly? Yes, but maybe only to
Eyrie Peak

Fees/Permits? None

Comment

Lewis Peak (8,031 ft) is located in North Ogden, Utah and sits on the mountain between Ben Lomond to the North and Mt. Ogden to the south. This peak is usually forgotten due to its popular neighboring peaks, but it is actually a very scenic summit. Lewis Peak was named after Lewis Warren Shurtliff, who was among the first known to summit this prominent peak. At the time, he was only 16 when he climbed what would be named Lewis Peak on June 6, 1852 with some friends. He piled up rocks on the summit and stuck a large branch in it to mark the high point. Lewis and his friends hiked here to scout out the area and help protect the settlers from the Native Americans. It's unusual for a geographic feature to be titled after a person's first name. In fact, Lewis Peak is only one of a few Ogden Wasatch Front Mountain peaks that is even named after a specific person.

Hiking Lewis Peak is perfect during Summer and Fall; it may be possible to hike here in Winter, but check the avalanche danger before heading out. In Spring, the trail can be extremely muddy. This is a great trail to do with your dogs off-leash. Be aware that motorized dirt bikes and mountain bikes also use this trail. The only shaded section is the first mile; after that, you are hiking along an exposed ridgeline which can become very windy.

Getting There

From SLC, head north on I-15 all the way to North Ogden. Take exit 349, and head East. Follow this as it turns into E 2600 N. Turn left at the light for 1050 E. Turn right on E 3100 N. This road leads you through a neighborhood where the speed limit is only 30MPH. As soon as you turn onto 3100 N, drive 3 miles up the narrow, winding road and look for the North Ogden Divide TH sign on your right. This is where you'll want to park and begin hiking. There is one restroom.

The Route

Park at the North Ogden Divide TH. The trail for Eyrie Peak & Lewis Peak starts on the south side of the parking lot by the big sign. Starting out, you'll be hiking on the Northside of the mountain. The first mile is all switchbacks, and because it's in the shade, it can be chilly. Hike up seven long switchbacks. Around 1.5 miles, the view really opens up and you can see into Eden and Huntsville, Utah and Pineview Reservoir. Across North Ogden Divide, you'll see the very long switchbacks heading up the mountain; this is one of the trails to Ben Lomond Peak. Bout 2 miles into the hike, you'll have your first view of Eyrie Peak to the left and your destination, Lewis Peak, to the far right. Reaching the trail split sign, continue straight for Lewis Peak. Eyrie Peak (8,136 ft) is technically the high point on your hike. Compared to Lewis Peak, Eyrie Peak is higher in elevation by about 100 ft. If you only had 1-3 hours to fit in a hike or run, this would be a good spot to turn around. Continue down the ridge. You can hike up, over, and down all the hills or skirt around the base of them. Continue following the trail as it leads you directly to Lewis Peak.

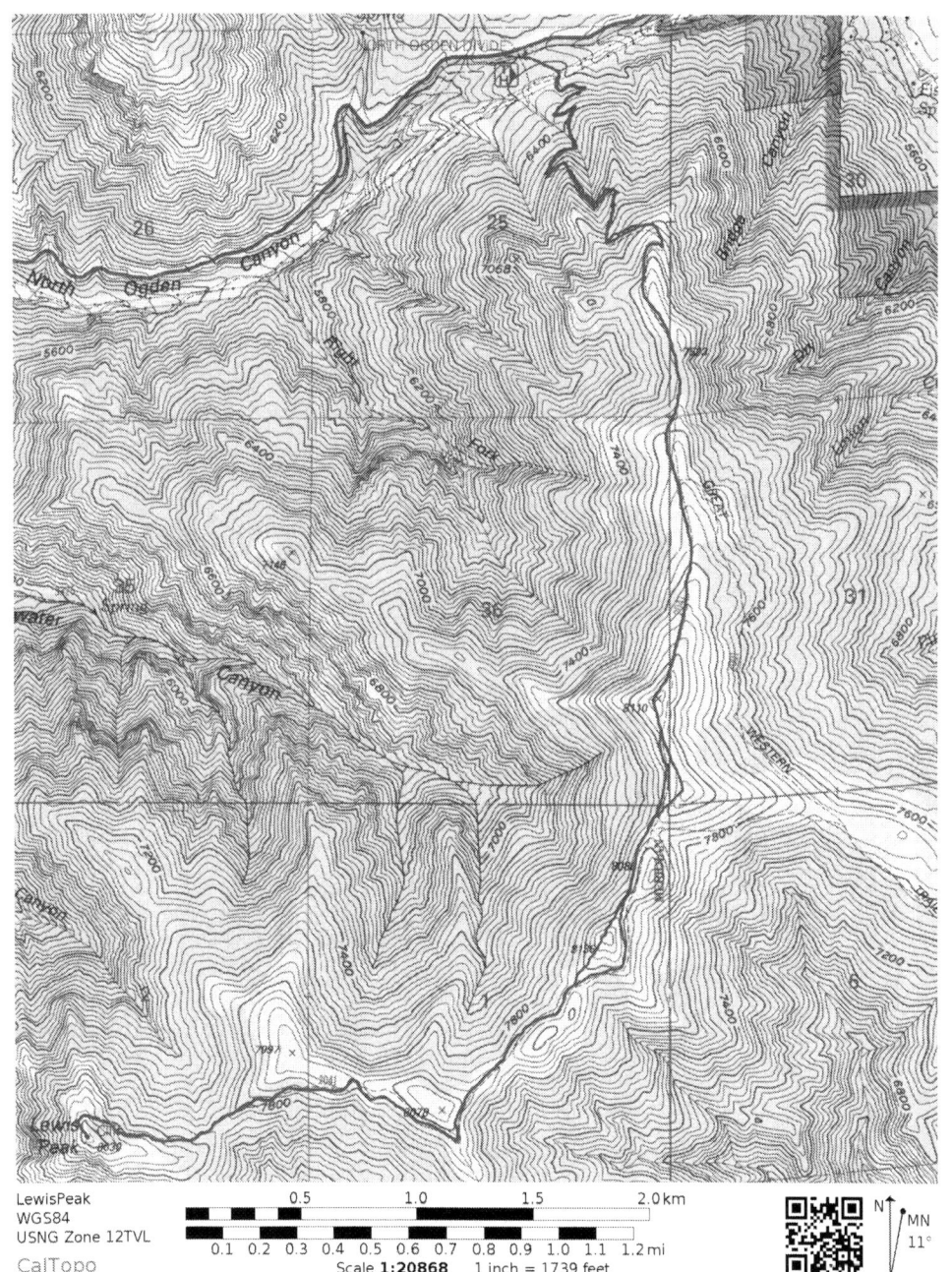

Grandeur Peak

Stats

Distance: 6 miles RT

Elevation gain: 2,900 ft

Time: 3-5 hours

Dog friendly? Yes. Dogs are allowed off-leash on odd days; dogs must be leashed on even days.

Kid friendly? Yes

Fees/Permits? There is a $5 fee upon exit, or FREE if you buy the Annual Millcreek Pass ($50). Millcreek Canyon does NOT accept the National Park Pass, American Fork Pass, nor the Mirror Lake Highway pass.

Comment

Grandeur Peak (8,299 ft) is one of the high points in Millcreek Canyon and offers fantastic views of the SLC Valley and into Parley's Canyon. Grandeur Peak is also a perfect intro to Peak Bagging - the fairly short trail with a moderate elevation gain makes it one of the easier peaks to the summit with little effort (compared to some of the other peaks in the area). For beginner hikers, this may be considered a tough hike due to the same reason Peak Baggers consider it easy - it is only 6 miles round trip and gains 2,900 ft elevation.

Grandeur Peak is a very popular trail and summit, so it's best to start early in the day to beat the crowds. The other nice thing about this trail is that it is safe to hike year-round. The south-facing slopes aren't of real danger during Winter, and the other seasons are just as spectacular. Because this trail is in Millcreek Canyon, dogs are allowed off-leash  on ODD days only. You can still take your dog here on EVEN days, but they must be leashed. This upper half of this trail is very exposed to sun and wind, so bring plenty of water for you and the dogs and sun protection. The ridge can get really hot in Summer.

Getting There

From SLC, head East on I-80, then take I-215 South. Take exit 4, then turn left. Turn left again onto Wasatch Blvd. At the next light, turn right, which will put you into Millcreek Canyon. Drive up the canyon until you reach the Church Fork sign, pointing left. This is where you'll need to park. The gate up the hill to the official TH is closed from Nov 1 - July 1. In Summer months, the gate opens at 8 am, which you could then drive up to the TH. However, every time I've hiked here, I've never been lucky enough to get a parking spot at the TH. In this case, park at the gate, then simply walk up the road to the TH. The restrooms are locked during winter.

The Route

Look for the Church Fork Picnic sign. You'll need to park on either side of the road, then walk up the road to the trailhead. Walk up the road, passing by a small waterfall. At the end of the paved road, you'll reach the official TH and upper parking lot. At the next 4-way intersection, you'll want to continue straight. The lower section of the trail is very well shaded and a stream runs along the right side. Perfect for the dogs to drink from! Climb up some stairs, and eventually, the trail will turn left. The upper half of the trail works up to several  switchbacks, and you'll now be fully exposed to the sun. Even though we hiked in late September, it was HOT on this section! In summer it worse because there is very little breeze until you reach the ridge. After many switchbacks, your last switchback is across several fallen rock piles. Once you reach the ridge, you can walk over to an overlook, which looks down into Parley's Canyon. Past this, the trail begins to get steeper. Make your way to the summit.

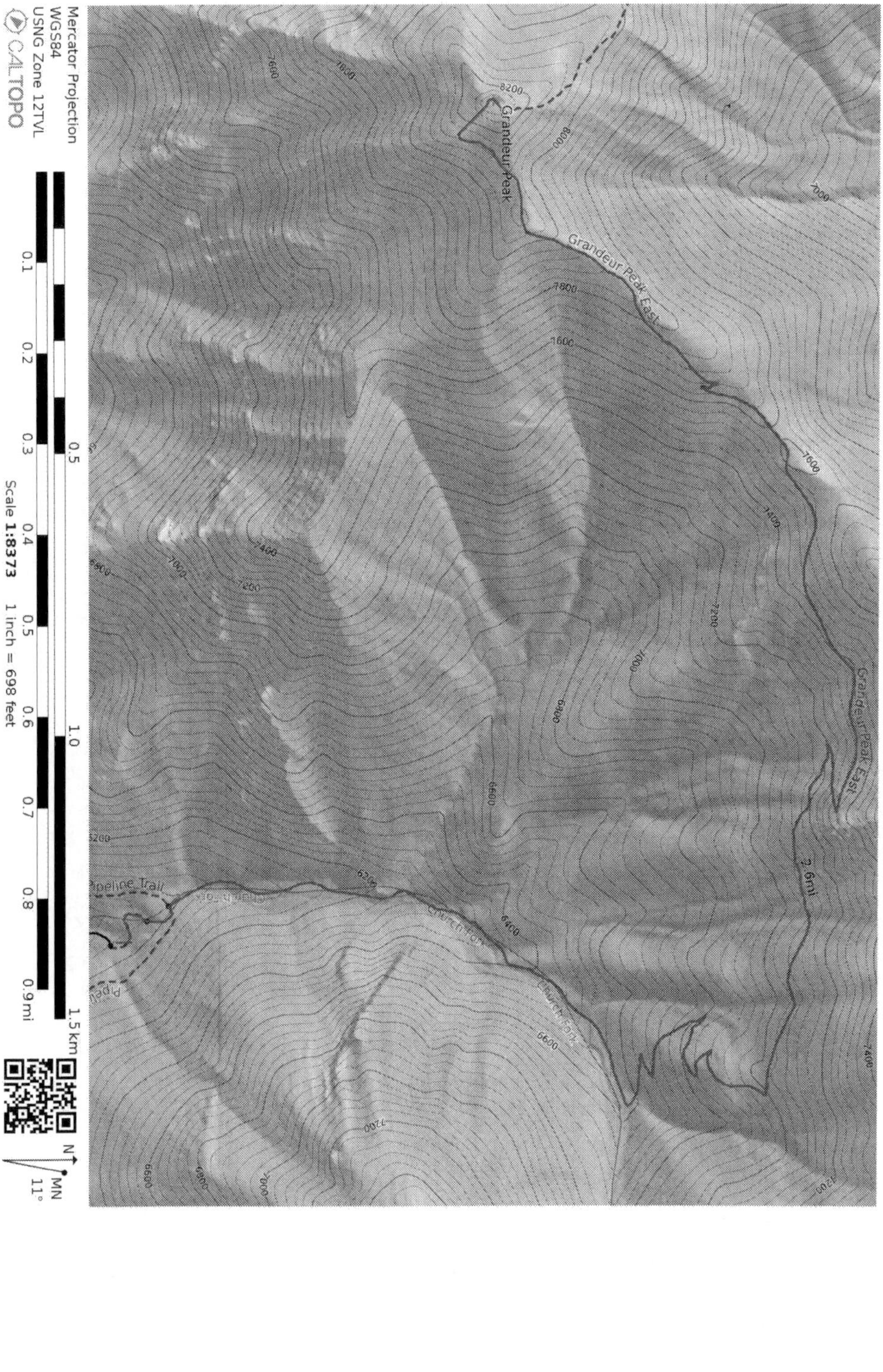
Mercator Projection
WGS84
USNG Zone 12TVL
CALTOPO
Scale 1:8373 1 inch = 698 feet
0.1 0.2 0.3 0.4 0.5 0.6 0.7 0.8 0.9mi
0.5 1.0 1.5 km
N
MN
11°
Grandeur Peak
Grandeur Peak East
2.6mi
Pipeline Trail
Church Fork

Spanish Fork Peak

Stats

Distance: 10 miles RT

Elevation gain: 4,600 ft

Time: 6-8 hours

Dog friendly? Yes, off-leash

Kid friendly? No

Best Season? Late summer & Fall

Comment

Spanish Fork Peak (10,192 Ft) stands out by itself; as you make your way down HWY 6 towards Price, UT, it sits in between two other big peaks (Provo Peak to the North and Santaquin Peak to the South). With almost 3,000ft of prominence, Spanish Fork Peak ranks #41 on the Utah Prominence Peak list and is higher than any peak in Weber and Davis counties. This trail is not for the beginner hiker — it climbs 4,600 Ft in just 5 miles. Steep is the name of the game, but your hard work will pay off with grand views of surrounding mountains and an alpine lake.

Getting There

From I-15 heading south from SLC, take exit 260 for W S 400 in Springville, UT, then head east. Turn right on Main St., then turn left W 800 N. Turn right onto N 300 W, then left onto E 400 N. Follow this all the way into Maple Canyon until you pass Whitings Campground. Drive to the very end of the road where the trail begins.

The Route

The trail starts at the most Eastern end of the parking lot. Walk past the gate. About 10 minutes up the trail, look for the bridge crossing the stream to your right, across from a metal bench. This is your turnoff for Spanish Fork Peak. The trail is well defined the whole way, yet rocky. Hiking poles are beneficial for a hike like this. The trail is very well shaded for the first half of the hike, and cuts through two small meadows. You will be following Trail 007 to get to the peak. Cross the stream once more. Up until this point, you will have hiked along the west side of the stream. After you cross this stream, you will be hiking on the East side of it for a while. About 1 mile before Maple Canyon Lake, the trail will open up. Walk around Maple Canyon Lake, and continue following the trail. Once you reach the ridgeline, head left. Continue following the ridge, then reach the summit marked by a triangulation tower.

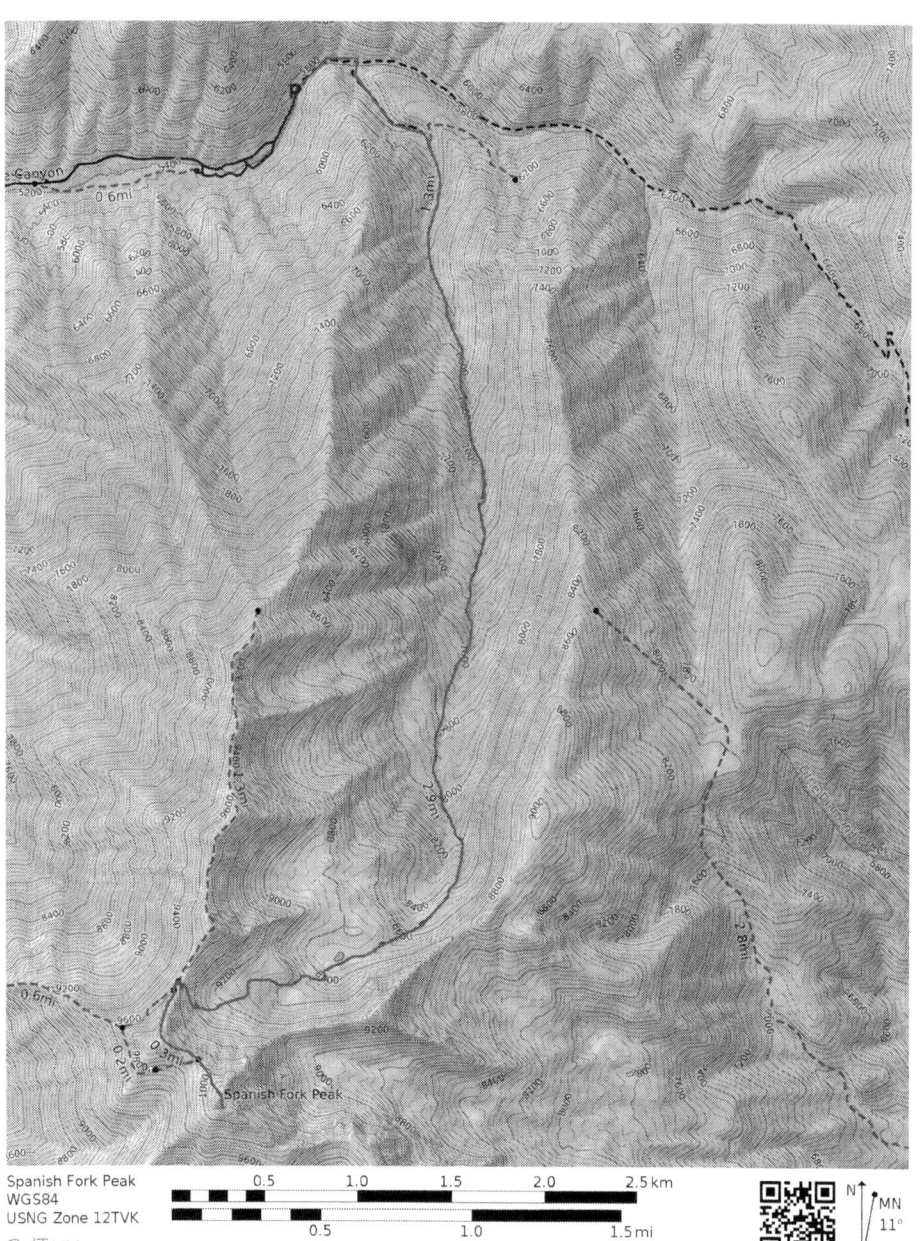

Spanish Fork Peak
WGS84
USNG Zone 12TVK
CalTopo

0.5   1.0   1.5   2.0   2.5 km

0.5   1.0   1.5 mi
Scale **1:25449**   1 inch = 2121 feet

N↑ ●MN
11°

Santaquin Peak

Stats

Distance: 11.2 miles RT

Elevation gain: 2,979 ft

Time: 6-8 hours

Dog friendly? Yes, off-leash

Kid friendly? No

Best Season? Late summer & Fall

Comment

Santaquin Peak & Loafer Mountain are the peaks above Santaquin, Utah and are in between the famous Mt. Nebo (tallest peak in the Wasatch) and Spanish Fork Peak. Though the trail leads to Santaquin Peak, Loafer mountain is 2 ft taller, yet not many people go off-trail to summit it. Santaquin Peak offers better views than Loafer Mountain, as you have 360-degree views of Utah Lake, Timpanogos and Provo Peak to the North, Mt. Nebo to the southwest, and on a clear day, you can even see Deseret Peak to the West. The first half of the trail is mostly forested, and the second half is fully exposed to sun and wind. Santaquin Peak has just under 3,000 ft of prominence.

Getting There

Head south on I-15 and take exit 250 in Payson, UT. Keep left on 3200 W, then left on E 100 N. Turn right on Nebo Loop Road. Reset your odometer here and drive 12.1 miles, where you'll see a pull-out for the TH on the left side of the road.

The Route

Once you park, you'll see this sign for 4 different trails. Head right for Loafer Mtn. It says 6 miles, but after tracking it, it was only 5.6 miles (one way). The first mile is very easy and very forested. Pass a small meadow within the first 5 minutes. At the first trail split, veer right. At the 2nd trail split - veer left. And at the 3rd trail split, turn right. The brown trail marker isn't well kept, but if you keep count of the trail splits, you'll know where/when to turn. The next 2-3 miles had very thick, dense low shrub. This is a section I wished I had pants on to protect my legs. However, it didn't last long. You can't even see where the trail is here. I felt like I was hiking in the wrong direction for this part. The trail leads us north, but I knew the peak was to the East. Eventually, the trail turns East and begins to get steep, and from this point on, there's no shade. It's also rockier compared to the first 2 miles. Work your way up the large switchbacks and ridge until you get to the saddle. Once on the saddle, continue right up to the next ridgeline. The last section of the trail is a little sketchy, as it's a little narrower, with loose rock. Watch your footing - one wrong step and you could easily slide off to the left.

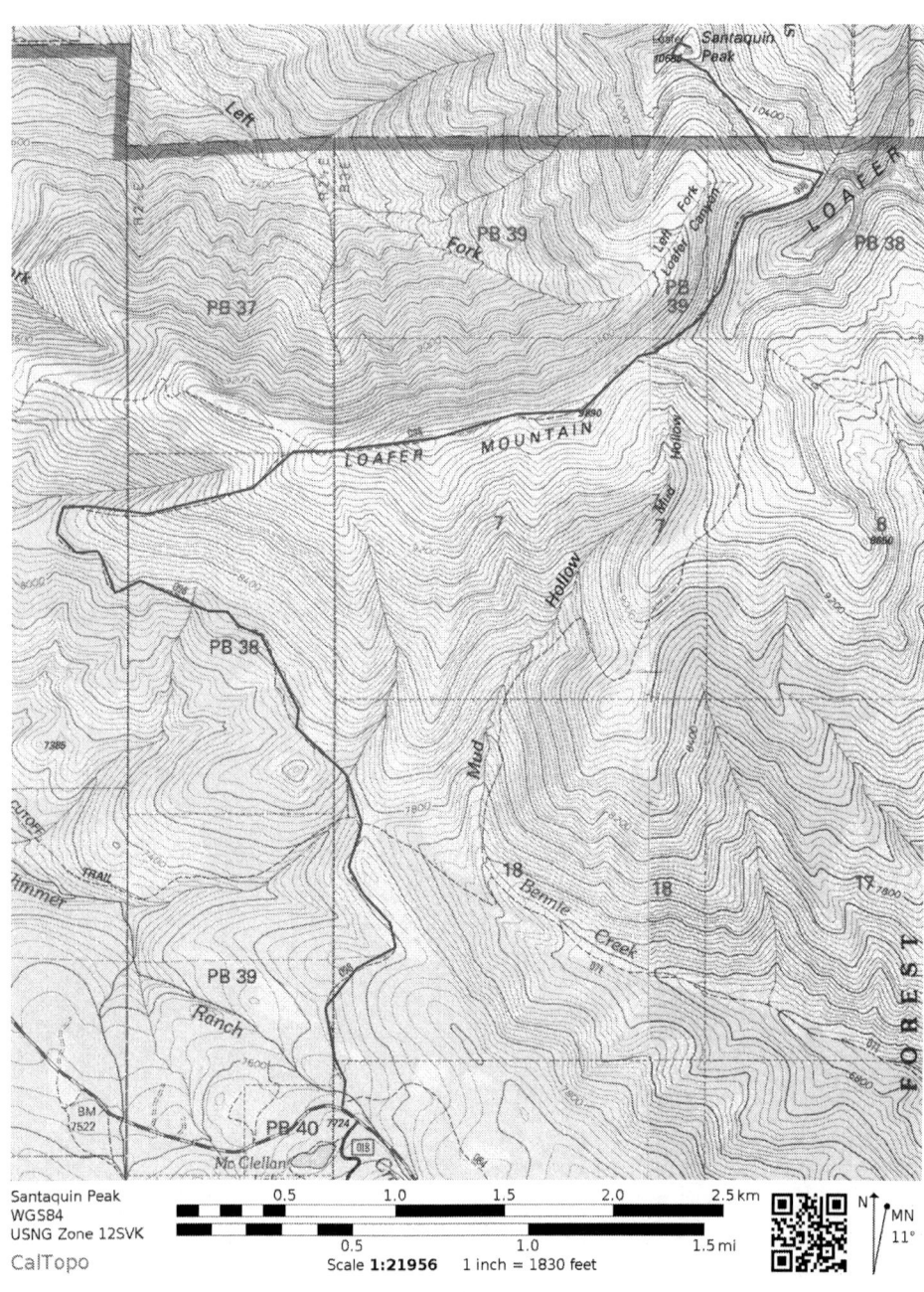

Santaquin Peak
WGS84
USNG Zone 12SVK

CalTopo

Scale **1:21956**   1 inch = 1830 feet

Lookout Peak

Stats

Distance: 10 miles round trip
Elevation gain: 2,900 ft
Time: 5-7 hours
Dog friendly? Yes, off-leash
Kid friendly? No

Comment

Lookout Peak sits at an elevation of 8,954 ft up Killyons Canyon in Salt Lake County. The summit is not the most spectacular, but the ridge on the hike offers amazing views of Parley's Canyon, Emigration Canyon, and City Creek Canyon. Although it is considerably lower in elevation compared to the more famous peaks of the Wasatch Front, Lookout Peak still rises over 4,000 ft above SLC. Though there is a well-defined trail, Lookout Peak gets much less traffic compared to other peaks. This peak would not be good to hike in spring or after a heavy rain/snow since it gets very muddy.

Getting There

In SLC, head north on Foothill Blvd, and turn right on Sunnyside Drive (this turns into Emigration Canyon Rd). Drive 6 miles, then turn left for Pinecrest Canyon Rd. Drive 1/4 mile, and park right before the road splits for Killyons and Pinecrest on the right side of the road. You should see the trail parking sign. You will then need to walk up 1 mile to reach the official TH.

The Route

Begin by walking up Killyons Canyon Road for 1/2 mile, where you still then reach the official trailhead. 10 minutes into hiking, you'll see the "Killyon Canyon Conservation Preserve" sign. Soon pass another sign, with everything pointing right. Gradually work your way up one switchback, then a small, tight gulley then you will come to a 4-way intersection. Head left (north) from here. If you go straight, it will take you to Affleck Park, and right follows the ridge south. Up on a small saddle, you will finally be able to see Lookout Peak. Continue following the trail as you start to gain more elevation and hike up another switchback, and then you will reach the main ridge. Once on the ridge, continue North, staying on the main trail. This peak is sneaky, making you climb over 4-5 false summits. Just when you think you are there - it keeps going! When you get towards the top, you will see the peak, which is a large, open meadow. Look for the small cairn on top and summit register.

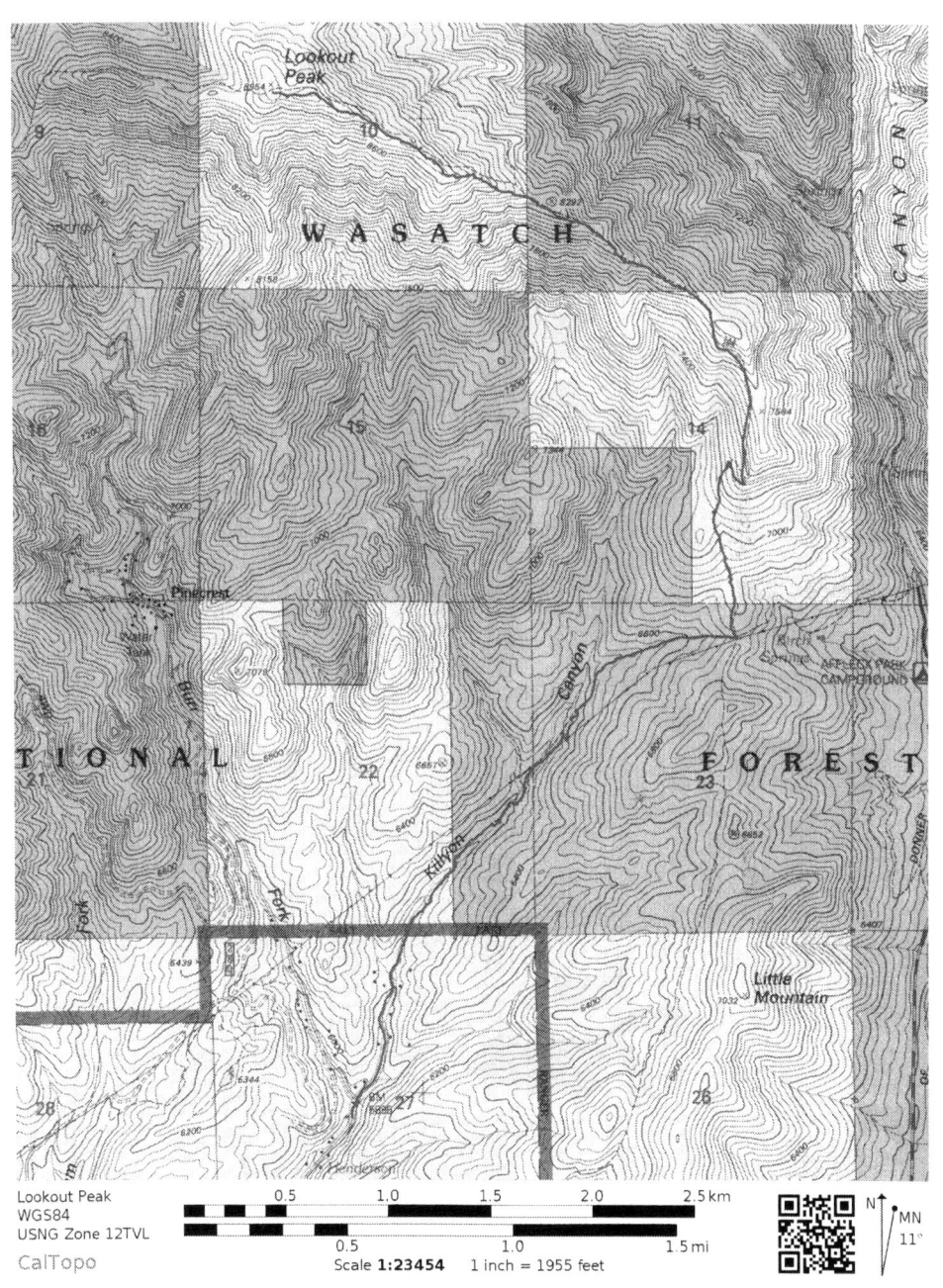

Scale **1:23454**   1 inch = 1955 feet

Mill Canyon Peak

Stats

Distance: 7 miles RT

Elevation gain: 1,954 ft

Time: 3-5 hours

Dog friendly? Yes, off-leash

Kid friendly? No

Fees/Permits? None

Comment

Mill Canyon Peak (10,349 ft) sits on the backside of the Wasatch Mountains and offers amazing 360-degree views. For a 10,000 ft peak, this is a relatively easy summit - there's a trail most of the way and no scrambling. You will likely not see another hiker which is great, but the biggest downside to this route is the number of dirt bikes. We passed seven of them by 9 am, and the noise and dirt they kicked up weren't the best, and I had to make sure I moved Charlie far enough off the trail. However, if you can get past that, you will get a huge reward in scenery and views on Mill Canyon Peak. This trail is only half-shaded, so you'll want to start early to beat the heat.

Getting There

Start by following the signs for Soldier Hollow from Midway/Heber. When you reach the "T", turn right onto Stringtown Rd. It will immediately cross a cattle guard and become a well-graded dirt road. Follow this for 7 miles until you reach Cascade Springs TH. Turn Right when you reach the second "T" at Cascade Springs. You should now be on a well-paved road, HWY 114. Drive 3.4 miles past Cascade Springs and look for the dirt road heading right (there's only one) with a sign for Mill Canyon Road. Drive to the very end of the dirt road where the TH starts on the right.

If you are coming from the Alpine Loop Road in American Fork Canyon, just follow the signs for Cascade Springs, then the Mill Canyon Road will be a left turn.

The Route

When you reach the end of the road, the trail starts to the right. You won't see any signs for Mill Canyon Peak - you will be following Ridge Trail 157. The trail is very dusty but gradually gains elevation for the first 2 miles. As you turn to head in a more East direction, you'll have your first view of Mill Canyon Peak. As you start to get higher in elevation, the trees disappear and you should have an amazing view of Mt.Timpanogos! As you turn a corner and head north, you can see exactly where you need to hike from here - follow the ridge all the way up. First, hike up and over a false summit. Now the trail is either very faint or non-existent at times. However, as long as you stay on the ridge, you'll make it. Eventually, you'll pick up a good trail again halfway up the ridge. This is also where I found the hike to be hardest since it's pretty steep. A good calf-burner! When you reach the false summit, you'll hike through a small area of boulders. Continue along the ridge (of and off a trail once again) until you reach the true summit.

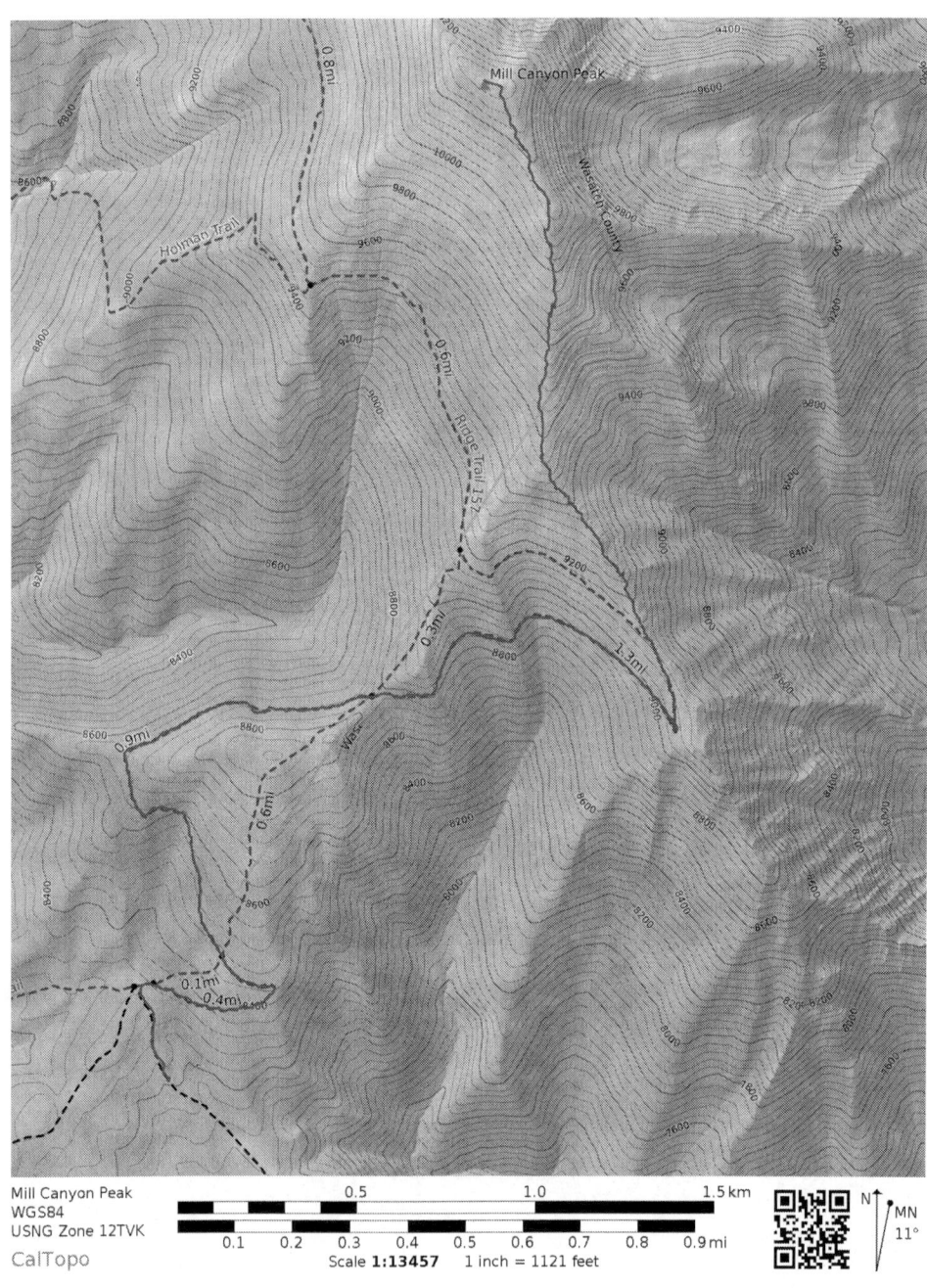

Mill Canyon Peak
WGS84
USNG Zone 12TVK
CalTopo

Scale **1:13457**   1 inch = 1121 feet

Fool Creek Peak

Stats

Distance: 6.7 mi RT (If you have a small car and have to park off the main road, it's 8.7 mi RT)

Elevation gain: 2,900 ft

Time: 4-6 hours

Dog friendly? Yes, off-leash

Kid friendly? No

Fees/Permits? None

Comment

Fool Creek Peak (9,712 ft) is the highest summit in the Canyon Mountain Range in central Utah and ranks #20 on the Utah Prominence List with 3,712 ft. I bet everyone has seen this peak, but nobody knows the name as you drive by it heading south on I-15 in Scipio, UT. This is one of the reasons I just had to hike this peak - every time I would drive on I-15, I said to myself, "One day, I'll hike to that peak!" So I did.

The summit of Fool Creak Peak is accessed from the West in Oak City, Utah. The drive is easy - even small passenger cars can drive up the canyon to a point. The terrain is a mix of desert and low brush. The forest fire from 2013-2014 really wiped out a huge section of this area. Surprisingly, there was quite a bit of new growth since then. The trees still have the burnt look, but the lower brush and oak have regrown. This brings me to an important tip - I highly recommend wearing pants for this trail. Parts of the trail are overgrown since it's not a popular hike, and it will scrape up your legs and make you itch.

Because the trees have not fully regrown, there is zero shade on this trail. Bring plenty of sunblock and water. There are three small stream crossings within the first 1/2 mile, but you are own your own after that. I carried 3L of water and put another liter of water in Charlie's dog pack. By the time we got back, all the water was gone.

Getting There

Drive south on I-15 and take exit 228 for Main St. in Nephi, UT and stay on this road for 2.8 miles. Turn right on HWY132 and stay on this for 28 miles. Turn left in Leamington, UT for HWY125 and drive 12.5 miles. In Oak City, UT, turn left on Center St., then Center St/L St turns right and becomes 200 E. Drive 5.7 miles to Oak Creek Canyon Rd.

The Route

After driving through Oak City, UT you will see the Fishlake National Forest sign. Soon you will see the Oak Creek Campground on your left. Drive another 1.7 miles to FR1653 (it's not signed, make sure you have a real map with you) and turn left here across this small creek up Walker Canyon as far as you can drive. This is where small, passenger cars will need to park because the road gets really rutted out. We reached the small brown sign that says "Trail 087 - Vehicles than 50 inches wide" and parked to the right on the dirt road.

This is where you also begin hiking. You'll cross three small streams within the first 1/2 mile. Perfect for the dogs to drink from. The first mile of the hike is along the ATV trail. At mile 1, you'll reach a small open gate. This is where ATVs are forced to turn around and where the trail turns into a single track.

You'll follow a dry wash for about 1/2 mile. I imagine if you hiked here earlier in the year, there would still be water here. Parts of the trail are overgrown since it's not a popular hike, and it will scrape up your legs and make you itch. The trail does get faint at times, but we never fully lost it. Two days later, my legs are still itching even though I had pants on. Hike up a few switchbacks, then read the saddle. From the saddle, you can look into the North Canyon. Keep right. You'll hike up and over a rocky section, then drop down to the second saddle. No scrambling is required. The hike up past the second saddle was the steepest, and where we lost the trail for 100 yards or so. It wasn't too hard to pick it up again if you stay along the ridge—lots of burnt trees. Hike up the last 4-5 switchbacks, then reach the summit, which is actually two summit markers on Fool Creek Peak as well as the triangulation tower.

Fool Creek Peak
WGS84
USNG Zone 12SUJ

CalTopo

0.5   1.0   1.5 km

0.1 0.2 0.3 0.4 0.5 0.6 0.7 0.8 0.9 mi

Scale **1:16116**   1 inch = 1343 feet

N
MN
11°

Mt. Elliott

Stats

Distance: 16 miles RT

Elevation gain: 2,842 ft

Time: 6-9 hours

Dog friendly? Yes, off-leash

Kid friendly? No

Fees/Permits? None

Comment

Mt. Elliott (7,142 ft) is located along the Book Cliff Mountains, in between Price, Utah and I-70. Ever driven to Moab from SLC? Then you've passed this peak and know exactly where it is! Near the town of Woodside, UT, there is an abandoned gas station with people sometimes selling jerky. Look directly up and SW, and you'll see this pointy peak clearly. You can't miss it; it sticks out because its jagged yet isolated summit. This obscure peak ranks #24 out of 29 on the Utah Country Prominence Peak list, and because of its low popularity, only a handful of people will make it to the summit each year.

Timing this peak is tricky. I'd say the hardest part is the Price River needs to be low enough to cross - typically, 50cfs or lower is ideal. I once planned to do Elliott in June, and during spring runoff, the flow rate was close to 200cfs! Obviously, I didn't end up hiking it that day. The other hard part is that you don't want it to be above 70-75F because there is hardly any shade and zero water along the trail. Dehydration and sunburn are the real deal in Southern Utah!

Because of this last part, I didn't want to bring Charlie along. I didn't want him to get too hot for 16 miles, have to carry a bunch more water for him, only for him to get sick, hurt a paw, or anything else. His max mileage these days is 12-14. Sadly, I left him home for this hike, even though dogs are allowed.

Lower flow rate and cool temps make Fall the ideal time to hike to Mt.Elliott! Be prepared with at least 3 liters of water, plenty of sunblock (we got sunburned even in October!), food, and other sun protection. Even though this hike is mainly on the road, the views on the summit of Mt.Elliott are worth it!

Side note: if you have an ATV or dirt bike, you only have to hike 1/2 mile to reach the summit.

Getting There

From Price, Utah, head south on HWY 6/191 for 37.8 miles (milepost 278) and you'll see an unsigned dirt road on your left (East side of the road) - turn here and reset your odometer. If you drive past the abandoned gas station, you went too far. This is also a good spot to turn around if you initially missed the  turn. At 4.3 miles cross a cattle guard, and at 5.2 miles, the road narrows to one lane; there is a brown sign off to the right, and is now considered a "jeep road", but as long as you have an SUV or larger, you can make it. Small cars will not appreciate the undercarriage getting hit by all the shrubs and banged up by rocks. At 7.9 miles, the road ends at the Price River. This is where we camped and parked for our trip, and there is a small turnaround.

The Route

Start by Crossing the river - be advised the water is cold even in Fall. We carried out hiking shoes and a towel across the river so that we could immediately change into our hiking shoes. We stashed our Chacos in some bushes, so we didn't have to carry them the entire hike. Having a trekking pole was helpful to gauge the water depth. We didn't cross right where the ATV road goes across because it looked deeper, so we crossed about 15 feet upriver from that and tried to stay on rocks. The water is very opaque and murky, and the mud is extremely sloppy. Don't be surprised if you fall in up to your knees or more, but also don't wear flip flops! Now the easy part begins - just follow the road up around the north end of a buttress. The road gets near the edge, and it's pretty cool to look down and see the Price River from above. That road is the one you should have driven in on. At 3.3 miles, we had our first sighting of Mt.Elliott! Only 4.5 miles to go! Most of the "hike" is a long, lonely road. In case you've been wondering, all these roads were built back in the 1970s for oil exploration! Not much came out of the expensive project, but it did lead to easier access for exploring this terrain. Finally, after walking on the road for 7.3 miles, it's time to route find your way to the summit. You'll see a large Juniper tree, and if you are tracking mileage, you'll know this is your turn. You'll be off-trail now but just aim for the saddle. It's not hard hiking this section, just a little steep. Reach the Mt.Elliott saddle! So cool to see the Swell and Highway 6 below. Stay left. There is some class 2 scrambling, depending on what way you climb up. Staying exactly on the ridge is impossible since there are cliff bands you can't climb up. It looks like the edge drops off, but it was never scary or too narrow. And finally, to reach the summit, there is one class 3 move. It's easy - we were both able to climb and up by ourselves without help from each other. Reach the summit and sign the register.

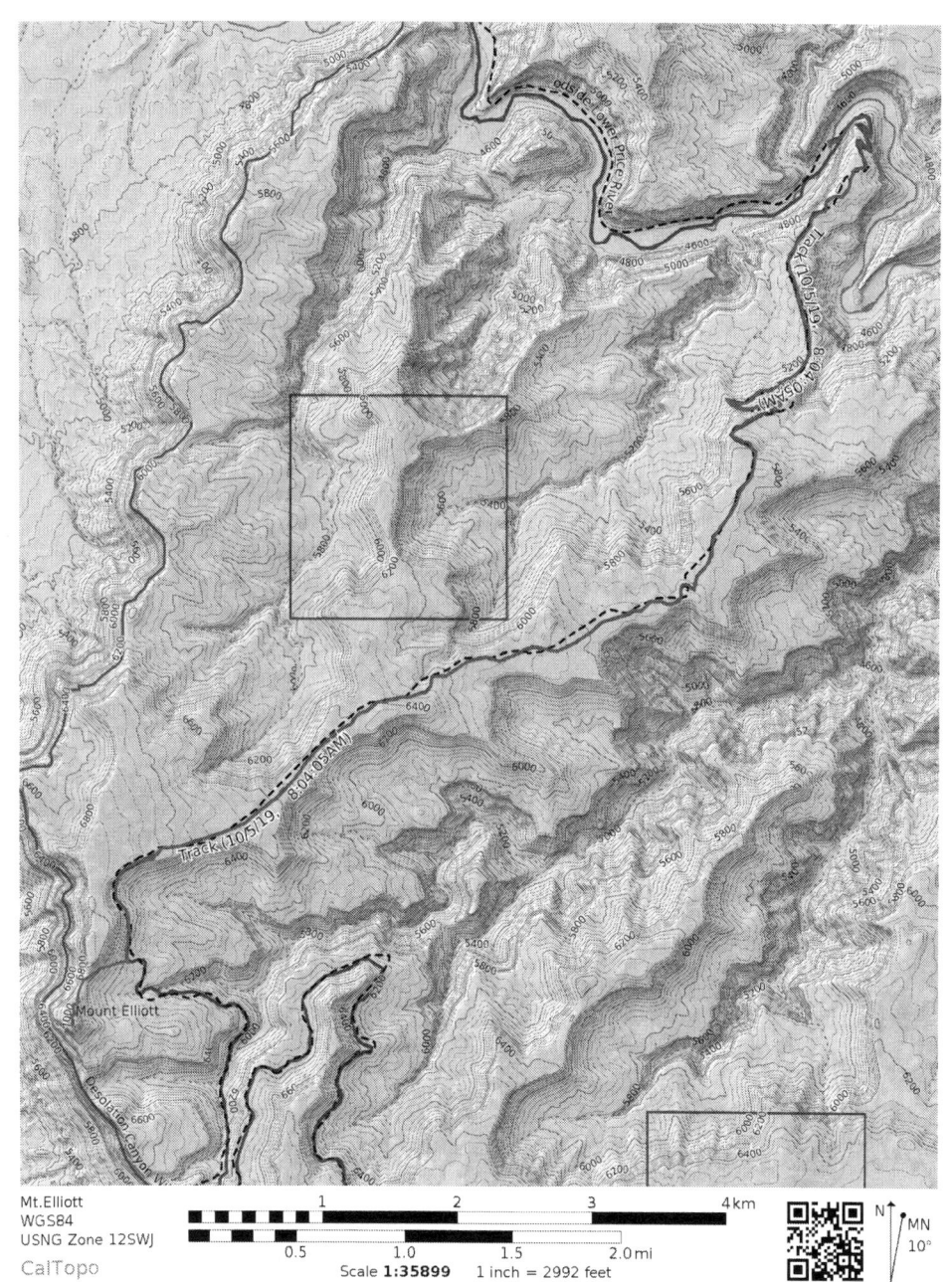

Lone Peak via Cherry Logging Trail

Stats

Distance: 15 miles RT

Elevation gain: 6,500 ft

Time: 8-12 hours

Dog friendly? No, dogs are not allowed

Kid friendly? No

Fees/Permits? None

Best Season? Late summer and fall

Comment

Lone Peak (11,251 Ft) is one of the tallest peaks along the Wasatch Front and hovers over Draper, Utah. You can't miss this peak — it is clearly visible from both Salt Lake & Utah Counties. On a clear day, you can see this magnificent summit from 100 miles away. Hiking Lone Peak is almost a rite of passage for many hikers and especially Peak Baggers. Although Lone Peak is not one of Utah's 8 Ultra Prominence Peaks, it does rank 98th on a list of Utah Peaks with 500 Ft of prominence and is on the list of the Wasatch 11ers (peaks over 11,000 ft). This intense hike is not for everyone - you must be very prepared for any kind of weather, and most importantly, prepared for a super intense hike that will take you all day. The hard work will be worth it though, as Lone Peak offers one of the best 360-degree views around.

Getting There

To get to the Cherry Canyon Logging Trail, you first need to get to the Orson Smith TH in Draper, UT. From SLC, head south on I-15 and take exit 291. Head east on 123rd south for 1.4 miles. Turn Right on 900 south, then Left on Pioneer Road. Continue straight around the Round-a-Bout. Turn Right on 2000 east. In 0.2 miles, you will see the Orson Smith Park/TH on your Left. This is where you will park. There are restrooms available. The Cherry Logging Trail starts to the left (north) and behind the restrooms up a set of stairs.

The Route

Locate the TH to the left of the restrooms and behind the info sign. Start hiking here. Hike up 4-5 easy switchbacks. Once you reach the large wide road, called the Aqueduct Trail, turn left. Then follow the signs to reach the Bonneville Shoreline Trail (BST). More switchbacks. At the next "T" you have reached the BST. Turn Left, following the Cherry Logging Trail sign, which is only about 75 yards away. You should see the sign for the Cherry Canyon Logging Trail and NO DOGS. Turn right (East) - the adventure now begins!

Work your way up another 6-7 steep switchbacks. The trail will level out for about 100 yards (already a relief)!, and briefly crosses Cherry Canyon, then aims up again. Just when you can't take any more switchbacks....There are about another 50 ahead of you. The trail wraps around the hillside, and again, offers a little relief from the steep hiking. The next 0.5 mile is relatively flat as it makes its way to a very small saddle and again climbs uphill. At 3.9 miles, you'll reach an obvious trail split marked by a cairn and stick in the middle. Stay left. Distance-wise, you are halfway. Time-wise, you still have another 4 hours of hiking from here. The trail drops into Bear Canyon for a little bit. This section is very forested and shaded. You'll pass one of the year-round springs to filter water. Climbing out of Bear Canyon will require about 10 more switchbacks. As soon as you climb out of Bear Canyon, you should see the Trail of the Eagle intersect the Cherry Logging Trail coming from the left (west). Stay on the main trail. Reach the Outlaw Cabin, built in 1960 by The Allen Brothers before this area were designated as a wilderness area.

The Cherry Logging Trail continues to the right (south) of the cabin and steeply gains elevation through a thickly forested section. In about 15 minutes, you should reach another ridge. 15 minutes or so past the Outlaw Cabin, you will reach a small ridge. The trail continues left along the base of what looks like a fingered, granite ridge. The trail is well marked by cairns, leading up to the next small ridge. Once you reach the small ridge, you will have your first full view of Lone Peak to the left and Box Elder Peak & Mt. Timpanogos to the South. The trail stays left, following cairns. Cross the meadow, and aim for one of the small drainages to reach the ridge. To reach the summit, the easiest way is to follow the North ridge. This is a good spot to drop your pack so you can hike lighter and faster to the summit. It will make for an easier scramble as well. If you do decide to keep your pack on, make sure everything is zipped into a pocket. Sunglasses, snack bars, or anything on the outside of your pack can easily fall out. Don't forget to put your camera in your pocket if you leave your pack behind. Continue following the ridge, getting narrower now, as you reach the summit!

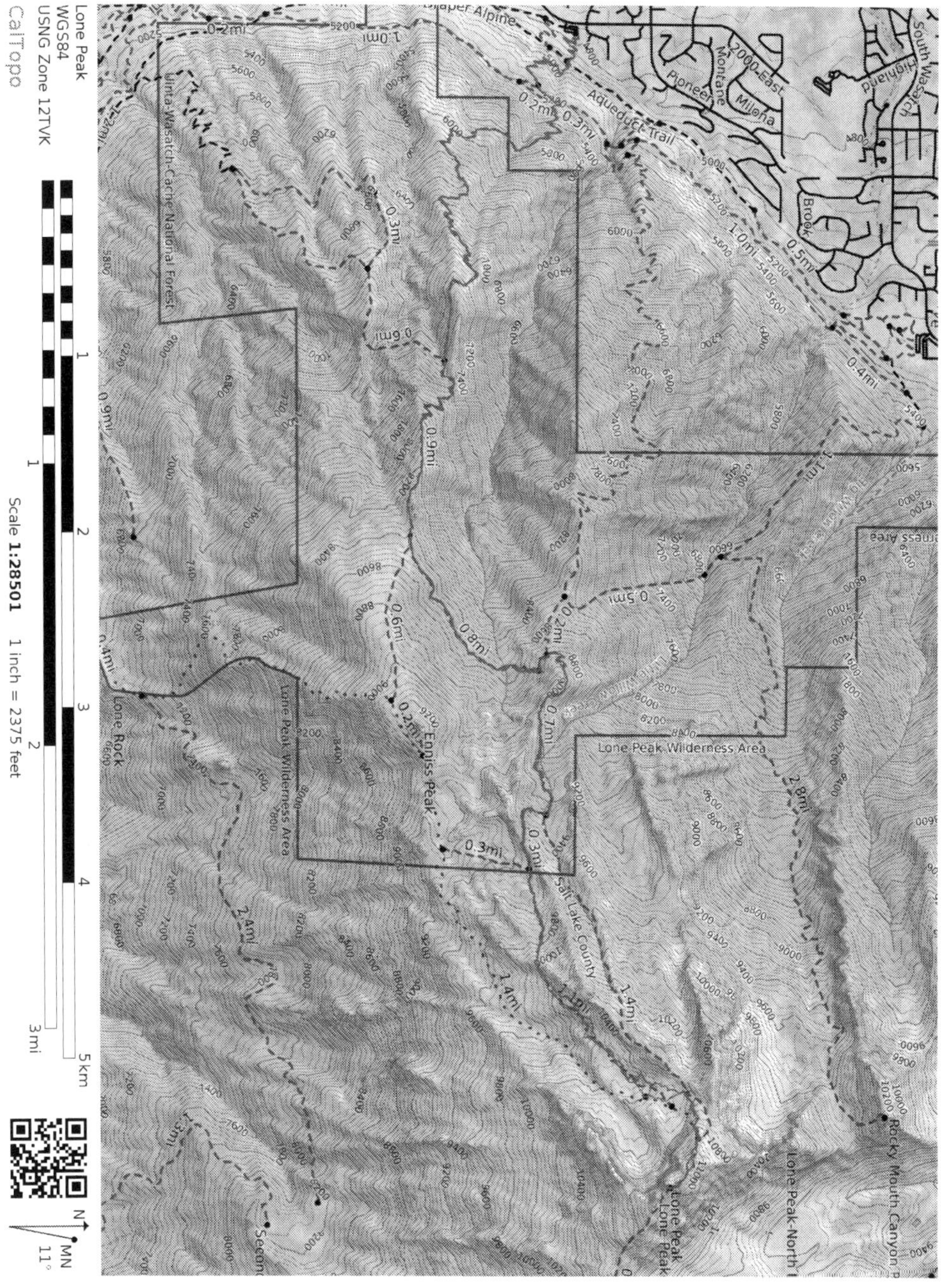

Lone Peak
WGS84
USNG Zone 12TVK

CalTopo

Scale **1:28501**   1 inch = 2375 feet

Uinta-Wasatch-Cache National Forest

Draper Alpine

Aqueduct Trail

Lone Peak Wilderness Area

Lone Peak Wilderness Area

Lone Rock

Enniss Peak

Salt Lake County

Lone Peak
Lone Peak

Rocky Mouth Canyon

Lone Peak North

N
MN
11°

Grandview Peak via Killyons Canyon

Stats

Distance: 18 miles RT

Elevation gain: 3,900 ft

Time: 10-13 hours

Dog friendly? Yes, off-leash

Kid friendly? No

Fees/Permits? None

Comment

Grandview Peak (9,410 Ft) sits at the Salt Lake/Davis County line and is one of the least seldom visited peaks along the Wasatch Front. It's a long hike in from all Getting There, there's no water source, very little shade, and a little bushwhacking required. No matter which route you choose (described below), be prepared for a full 10-12 hour day. However, I've been staring at this peak for 4 years now, and I just HAD to knock it off my peak list. Wednesday night I was looking at the weather for the week, and it was supposed to have perfect blue skies, comfortable temperatures, and the fall colors were also almost at their peak.

Getting There

From SLC, head east on 8th south until it turns into Sunnyside Drive. Continue past Utah's Hogle Zoo for 6.2 miles and turn left at the sharp curve in the road for Pinecrest Canyon. Parking will be on your right both immediately and about 0.2 miles further up the road marked with a tall white/green parking sign. If you reach the "Y" in the road, you went too far.

The Route

Begin by walking up Killyons Canyon Road for about 1/2 mile. Dogs need to be on a leash while on the road. Reach the trail, then dogs can be off-leash. As you hike up the trail, you'll pass a sign, "Killyons Canyon Conservation Reserve" within the first 15 minutes, then cross two bridges. The trail is very mellow for the first mile and gradually follows a small gully. When you reach the first 4-way intersection, turn left, and you'll make your way to the ridge. As you hike along the ridge, keep an eye out for a faint trail split to the right. This is your turn. Going straight will lead you to Lookout Peak. After you take the trail split, you will hike through several Aspen groves and weave in and out of the NE hillside for the next 2 miles. Reach a small unnamed peak — this is your first really good view of Grandview to the NW. Around 5.8 miles, you'll take the trail split left and head downhill on the hill's north side. At the bottom of the hill, and now you'll hike up a few switchbacks to reach the next ridge. It gets really overgrown through this section, but it's always easy to stay on the trail.

Once on the ridge, it's easy ridge walking for another mile. You'll continue following the trail as it starts to wrap around to the North. It will feel as if you missed the next trail split to the NE ridge of Grandview but keep going until you see it split. Hike by a red dirt patch, and the trail will cross this and continue along the NE ridge. From here, the trail seems to favor the West side of the ridge as there is a decent trail the whole way to the peak. You'll reach a really small saddle, and from there, stay on the East side of the ridge following this rock wall. It will get really steep the last little bit. Reach the summit!

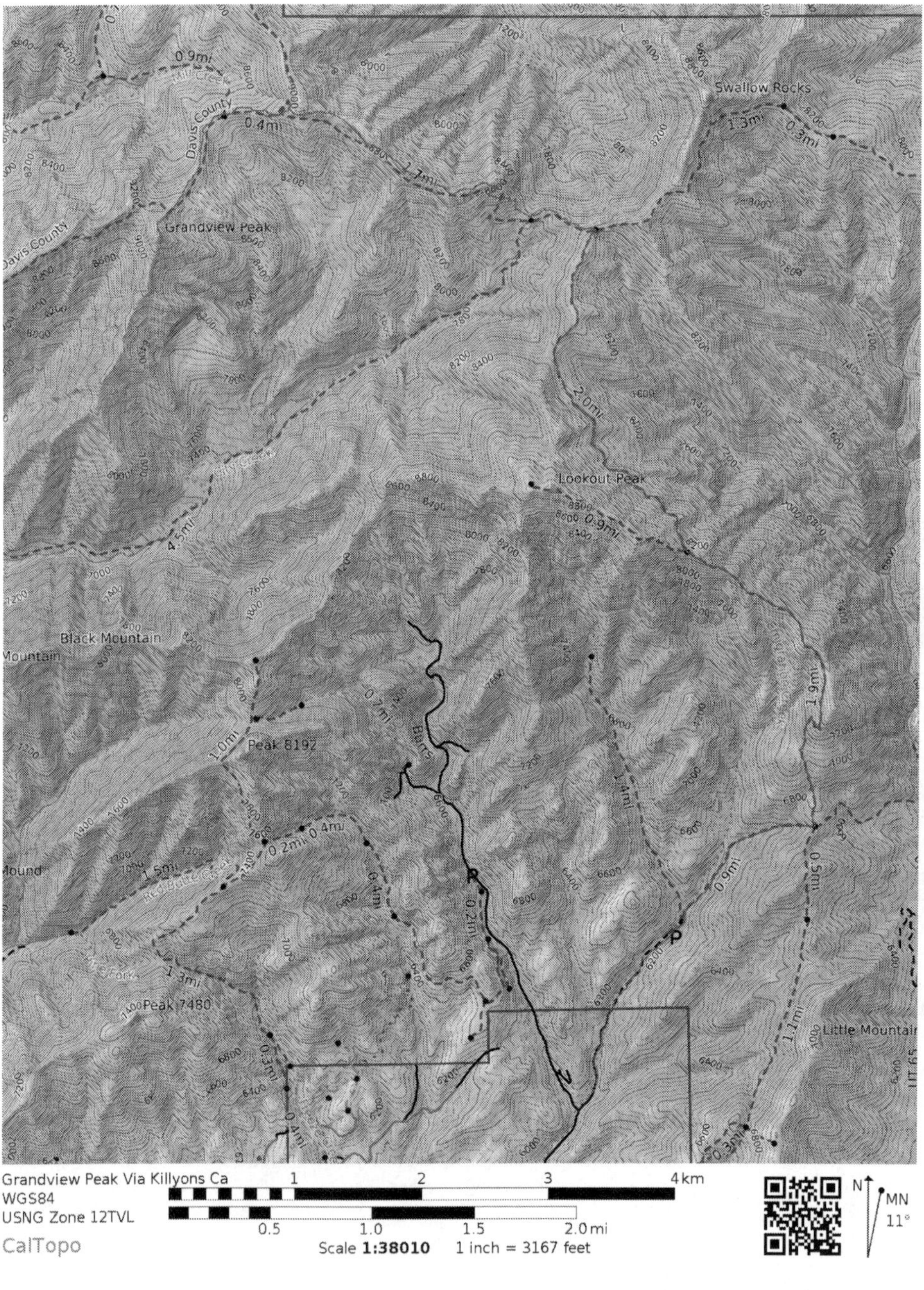
Swallow Rocks
Davis County
Grandview Peak
Lookout Peak
Black Mountain
Peak 8192
Peak 7480
Little Mountain
Grandview Peak Via Killyons Ca
WGS84
USNG Zone 12TVL
CalTopo
Scale 1:38010 1 inch = 3167 feet
MN
11°

Provo Peak

Stats

Distance: 3 miles RT

Elevation gain: 2,700 ft

Time: 2-4 hours

Dog friendly? Yes, off-leash

Kid friendly? 12+ for teens who
already have some peak
bagging experience

Fees/Permits? None

Best season? Late Summer and fall

Comment

Provo Peak (11,068 ft) is one of the higher peaks in the Wasatch and one of the shortest but steepest areas. The trail to the summit is only 1.5 miles but gains 2,700 Ft! The views from the summit are amazing, as you get 360-degree views of Utah County, and on a clear day into SLC County and major peaks north. Provo Peak is one of the "Wasatch Seven" peaks many peak baggers like to summit, as its one of the more prominent looking peaks. It's rare that such a massive peak gets less attention that its popular neighbor hikes like Squaw Peak and The Y Trail, but it's the case here. While there is a well-defined trail to the summit, Provo Peak sees way less traffic compared to neighboring trails/summits.

Getting There

Head south on I-15 from SLC, and take exit 272 for W 800 N in Orem, UT. Continue east, then take 189 north. Drive 2 miles, then turn right on FR027. Follow this road all the way to the trailhead.

You do need 4x4 or high clearance to reach this trailhead. Though it's only about 13 miles from the turn off of HWY 189, it will take about an hour to drive there since the road is so rough and can be rutted out. The Squaw Peak Road is only open around June (or whenever the snow melts) to October 31st. Small cars can drive all the way to the turn off for Rock Creek Campground. Past that is where you need 4x4.

The Route

You'll know you are at the trailhead when you reach the pass and see a loop in the road off to the right (west). Park here. The trail to Provo Peak starts by walking up the dirt road heading east. Eventually, this road will narrow, get rockier, and become covered by fallen trees. About 10 minutes up the route, keep an eye out for the cairn. Turn right here, and start hiking up the small, single-track trail. The trail can get overgrown in parts, but it's never hard to lose the trail. The trail turns from dirt into rock and scree. You'll reach three distinct false summits. You'll know you are at the summit when you see the metal wind vane.

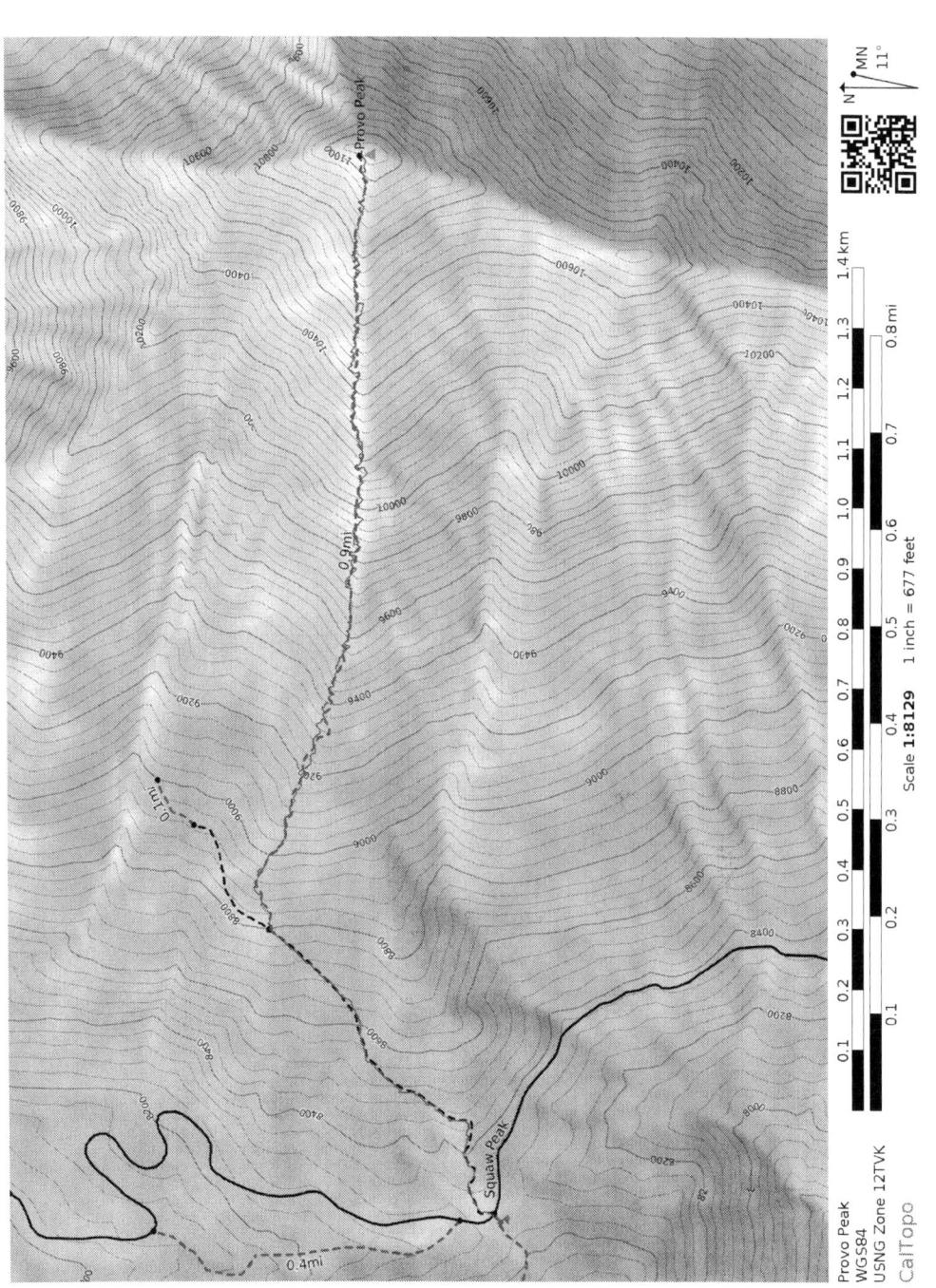

Provo Peak
WGS84
USNG Zone 12TVK
CalTopo

Scale **1:8129**   1 inch = 677 feet

Mt. Timpanogos via Aspen Grove

Stats

Distance: 15 miles RT

Elevation gain: 4,800 ft

Time: 6-8 hours

Dog friendly? Yes, off-leash

Kid friendly? Yes, older kids

Fees/Permits? There is a $6 fee for entering the Alpine Loop Road, or FREE if you have the annual National Park Pass or the annual American Fork Canyon pass. No permit is required.

Comment

Hiking Mt. Timpanogos (11, 752 ft) is one of the higher peaks in the Wasatch Front, coming in second behind Mt. Nebo. Though Mt. Nebo is the tallest peak in the Wasatch Mountains, it sees less than half the amount of hikers than "Timp" (as us locals call it) does. Hiking Mt. Timpanogos is almost a  rite of passage for many Utahans - once completed, many will openly offer up their experience, advice, and how many times they've summited.

For many hikers, Timp is done at least once a year - for others, over hundreds of times. Ben Woosley, one of the most famous and oldest Timp hikers, had signed the summit register for his 812th time on my visit! Many people like to hike up super early (think midnight or 1 am) to watch the sunrise over the Eastern ridgeline or camp in one of the many meadows, then wake up early and hike the rest of the way up to the peak. No matter what time of day you hike it or how many times you've done it, always be prepared with plenty of water, food, sunblock, hat, etc. Hiking Timp typically takes hikers 6-8 hours round trip, and there's not much shade. In summer months, I definitely recommend bringing a water filter, such as the Sawyer Mini, in case you or anyone in your group runs out.

Dogs are allowed off-leash. However, only bring your dog if they hike frequently and are used to that high of mileage and elevation gain. Dogs also need at least 2 Liters of water, so if you have a backpack for them, they can carry their own water. If they don't have a backpack, plan on carrying 4-5 liters for water for you and your dog. As for kids, I have seen babies in backpacks and some younger kids too. Just like with dogs, kids should have plenty of hiking experience under their belt and be able to carry their own water and snacks

Getting There

To get to the Aspen Grove trailhead from SLC, head south on I-15. Take exit 272 for 800 South in Orem, and head East. Drive straight on 800 S for 3.7 miles, then turn into Provo Canyon. Drive another 7 miles until you see the sign for Sundance Ski Resort, and turn left. Drive-up this road for 2.6 miles, and drive past the fee station for the Alpine Loop Road. Immediately after the fee station, turn left into the large parking lot. There are restrooms available.

The Route

Start by parking in the Stewart Falls parking lot, just to the left after the American Fork Canyon entrance. The Aspen Grove trail to Timp starts in the NW corner of the parking lot and heads in a Westerly direction the whole route. 5 minutes after hiking, you'll pass the TERT Station (Timpanogos Emergency Response Team), with the trail register. At the
first trail split, turn left. At 1 mile, pass First Falls, a nice waterfall. The trail makes several switchbacks up the Primrose Cirque. There will soon be an exposed rock side area. The trail is very well defined and solid - no need to worrying about sliding off the edge. At about 4 miles, the trail reaches the next ledge on the mountain and flattens out a bit. If you bring your dog, bring a leash in case mountain goats are on the trail. Thankfully, Charlie will just sit and stare

or sometimes bark when he sees wildlife - he's not a chaser. If you have a chaser, bring a leash! Depending on how wet of a Spring Utah had, you may pass several more small waterfalls. At mile 5, you will pass by Emerald Lake, a great spot to take a break and refill water if needed, and right on the trail. Big two no no's!

You'll see a large snow patch above Emerald Lake - this is what some people refer to as the "glacier" on Timp. At mile 5.5, you'll reach the shelter. Past the shelter, you will hike through a large boulder field - look for cairns and follow the most well-worn path until you reach the saddle on the ridge. Near this is where the more popular Timpanokee Trail intersects with the Aspen Grove Trail. Once on the saddle, you will have your first great views down into Utah County and Utah Lake. Turn left. Work your way up the rocky ledge, following cairns. You'll hike up several more mini switchbacks. Even in the middle of summer, I recommend bringing a light jacket for this section. The summit can get very windy and cold. If you've been sweating a lot from the hike, you will cool off very fast. Continue following the trail until you reach the summit, marked by a white shelter and summit register.

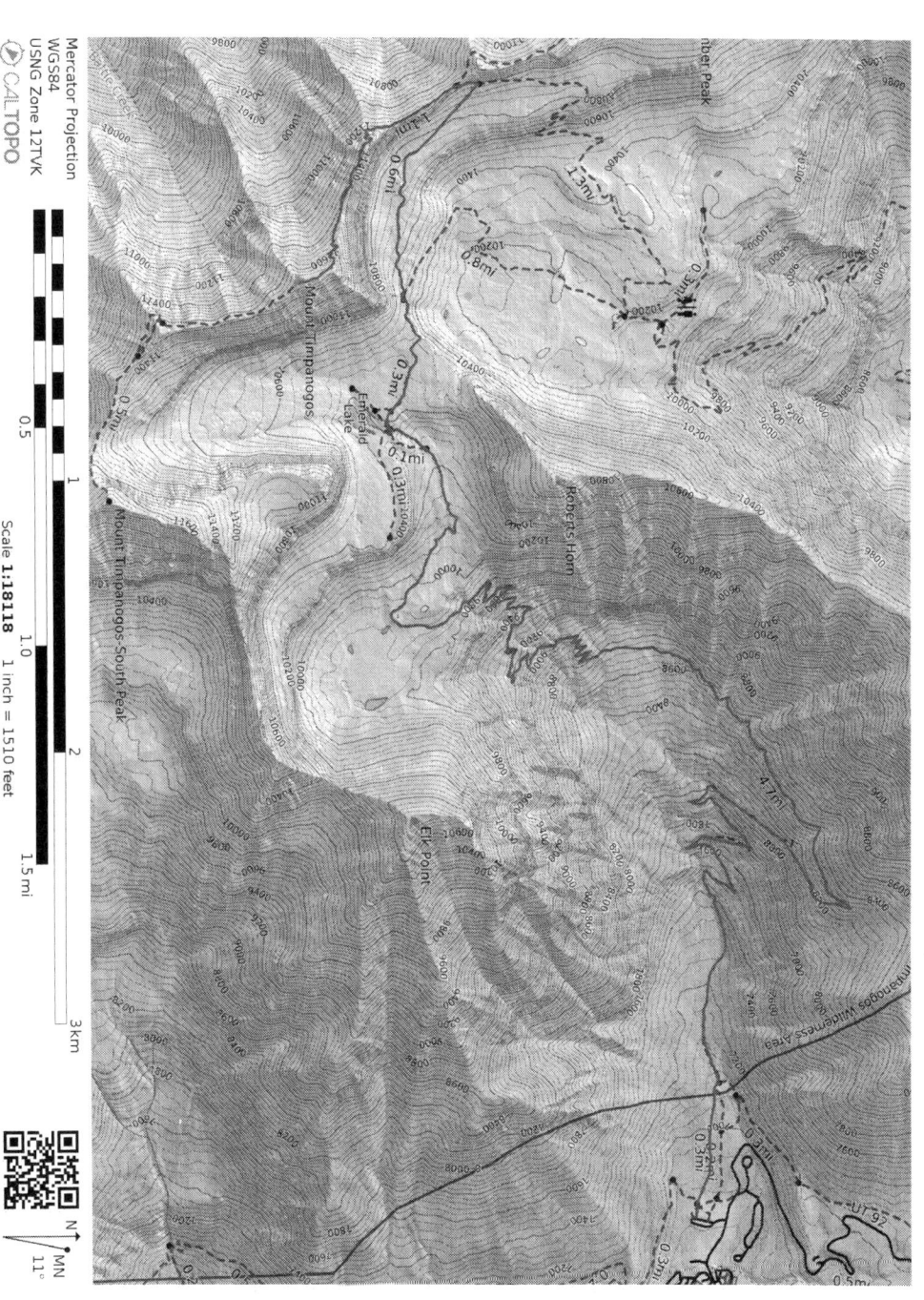

Wellsville Cone

Stats

Distance: 10 miles RT

Elevation gain: 3,200 ft

Time: 6-8 hours

Dog friendly? Yes, off-leash

Kid friendly? No

Fees/Permits? None

Comment

The Wellsville Cone (9,356 ft) is the 2nd highest point in the Wellsville Mountains, the highest being Box Elder Peak. Wellsville Cone is only 16 feet lower, and if you must bag the tallest peak of the mountains, go for it, but the views will be the same. There are several routes to reach either summit and all require bushwhacking and are long, steep hikes. This trail is 10 miles RT and gains 3200 ft elevation and the shortest route. The TH starts on the East side of the range near the town of Mendon. There are three long sections of major bushwhacking. The trail is always visible in Fall; however in summer, when the trees are in full bloom, it will be very easy to lose the trail. I highly recommend you go in late fall to be able to see the trail.

Getting There

To the Cold Water Canyon/Maple Bench TH

If you are driving from SLC, head north on I-15 and take exit 362 towards Logan, UT. Drive through the canyon for16.5 miles and turn left at the small sign for Mendon, UT. Drive through the small town of Wellsville and from HWY 23, turn left on 5400 West/Main St (it's another

really small street sign, so be on the lookout. If you drive into town past S 200 W, you went too far). Once you make the sharp left turn onto 5400 W, immediately turn right at the next road, which turns into a dirt road. You'll drive be several large homes. From here, keep following the dirt road until it ends at the TH. You'll pass the national forest sign and cross one cattle guard - I've marked both on the map below. Using Google Maps doesn't work because it doesn't recognize the endpoint/trailhead. Most cars should be able to make it. Small cars will have to drive slowly. It also depends on road conditions - if it's muddy, you'll either need 4x4 drive or just walk up the road, but it does add on an extra 3-4 miles one way.

The Route

As you drive along the dirt road, you'll pass the winter gate, which closes November 15th. Keep driving until you reach the end of the road. The trail starts behind the wood sign, and you'll hike in a southerly direction for the first mile. Pass Coldwater Lake - It's really a mucky pond 50 ft long by 15 ft wide. Keep an eye out for the nice trail sign, and turn right. You will begin hiking uphill. The first section has a lot of bushwhacking. It was so thick I could barely see Charlie. I really don't know how you'd be able to find the trail in Summer when everything is blooming and covered with leaves. Make sure you wear pants and long sleeves on this route to protect your skin from getting cut up and don't wear your "nice" hiking clothes. Hike up several switchbacks. Finally, when the trail opens up, you really do get nice views. There were three false ridges, that when you got to them, you just felt like you hadn't even hiked very far. Eventually, you will reach the true ridge, which has a large brown sign. Stay left. When we hiked along the ridge, we all thought the first peak you see was the cone, but it's not. You'll hike around it to the other side, where the trail keeps going. Reach another sign for Wellsville Cone! I thought it was really interesting that there were such nice, new-ish trail signs, yet the trail itself was in poor condition. You'll hike up a few more switchbacks when you get close to the summit. Reach the true summit marked by a small pile of rocks.

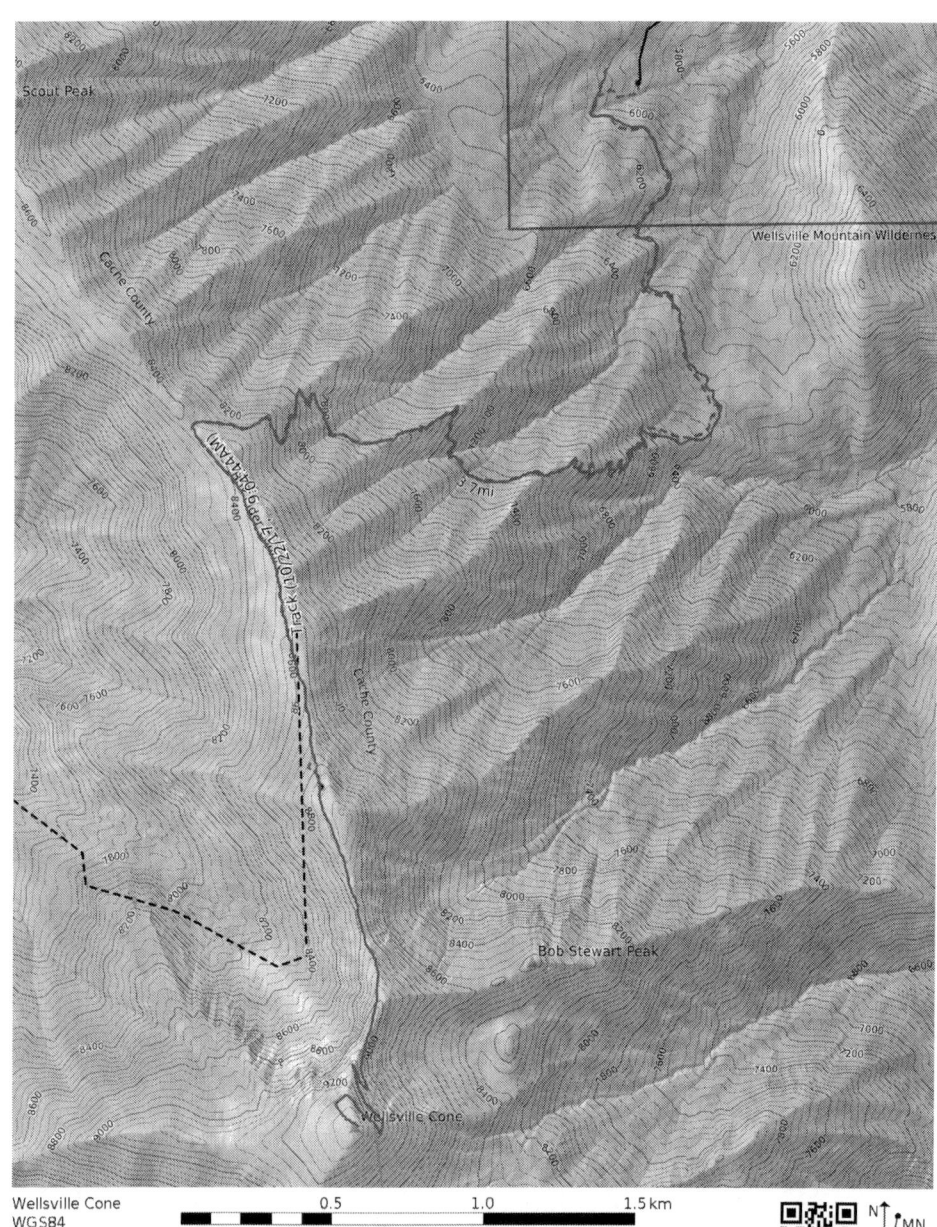

Wellsville Cone
WGS84
USNG Zone 12TVM
CalTopo

Scale **1:16012**   1 inch = 1334 feet

Box Elder Peak

Stats

Distance: 14 miles (loop) .

Elevation gain: 5,100 ft

Time: 6-8 hours

Dog friendly? Yes, off-leash

Kid friendly? No

Fees/Permits?

There is a $6 fee for a 3-day pass to enter AF Canyon. If you have an annual National Park Pass or annual AF Canyon Pass it is free. No permit is required.

Comment

Box Elder Peak (11,101 ft) is the large, well-known peak in between Mt. Timpanogos and Lone Peak - it dominates the ridgeline above and to the North of American Fork Canyon. Because the summit is over 11K, it is a popular hike among Peak Baggers. There are several routes to choose from, the most popular being the Dry Creek-Deer Creek Trail #043, which starts from the Granite Flats Campground just past Tibble Fork Reservoir.

The best way to hike Box Elder Peak is to turn it into a loop hike, so you get to see more of the mountain and experience a new trail. The route isn't for the beginner hiker though - the long, steep trail is sure to give your calves a workout and leave you out of breath. On the way to the summit, the trail gains 4,900 ft in just 7 miles - whew! There is no water along the trail, so be prepared to carry at least 3 liters of water, plus more if you bring your dog. Another plus about hiking Box Elder - dogs are allowed off-leash.

Only dogs with a lot of hiking experience in rocky, rough terrain and who have done several high mileage hikes should attempt this hike. On average, Charlie and I hike 15-20 miles a week, so he's used to doing hikes this long. If your dog has never done more than 10 miles in one day without issues (paws tearing, dehydration, soreness, etc), this is not the hike for them. Dogs will need at least 1 liter of water on this hike.

Box Elder Peak is best to summit in Summer or Fall. Winter and Spring will be sketchy due to snow and avalanche terrain and may require crampons and an ice axe - only very experienced mountaineers should attempt Box Elder in Winter.

Getting There

From SLC, head south on I-15 and take exit 284 towards American Fork Canyon. You will now be on HWY 92 - drive into the canyon past the fee station. Turn left at the brown sign for Granite Flats Campground & Tibble Fork Reservoir. Drive this road for another 2 miles until you reach the reservoir. Just past the reservoir is a sharp left turn, which heads up the hill. Continue for about 1 mile until you reach the campground. If the campground gate is open (after 8 am), you can park at the TH, which is about 100 yards past the entrance on the right. If the gate is locked, you can park just before the campground, on the right. There is enough space for about 4-5 cars in each area.

The Route

Parking is just before the campground entrance on the right. If the gate is open, you can drive through and park at the actual TH, also on the right, about 100 yards up the road. Walk up to the official TH for the Dry Creek-Deer Creek #043. The first 1.5 miles is pleasant through a forested area. You'll cross  the dirt road twice. Be careful of cars and ATVs flying down this road. At 1.8 miles, you hit the first of many switchbacks. This is also when the trail begins to really gain elevation. Hike up Switchbacks through an Aspen grove. The trail doesn't lead directly to the main saddle. It actually takes you up higher on the ridge to a flat meadow to a 4-way intersection. First, you will cross through a white boulder field. Reach a 4-way intersection. To get to Box Elder Peak, you'll want to continue straight along the ridge. From this point to the summit, it took me another 1.5 hours. Continuing down the ridge, you'll reach a trail split. To reach the summit, go straight, and the trail becomes extremely steep.

This trail split is where you'll want to return to and turn at, if completing the loop as I am describing here. The trail was very steep, and this stretch from the saddle to the peak is the hardest section of the trail. The trail to the summit stays on the West side of the ridge. Reach the summit! After summiting Box Elder, head back down to that last un-signed trail split, and follow it downhill from the saddle. This trail turns into White Canyon Trail (however, you won't see any signs for it for the next 2 miles or so). When you are hiking down this, you can see the Dry Creek-Deer Creek trail you hiked up across the canyon. The track does get a bit overgrown at times, but it's never hard to stay on the correct trail. Eventually, you'll reach a signed trail split. Turn left here, and you are now on the Box Elder Trail #044. This route is another option for summiting Box Elder if you turn right. Pass by an old miners cabin on the right. Then you'll be back at the campground. Make your way through it back to your car.

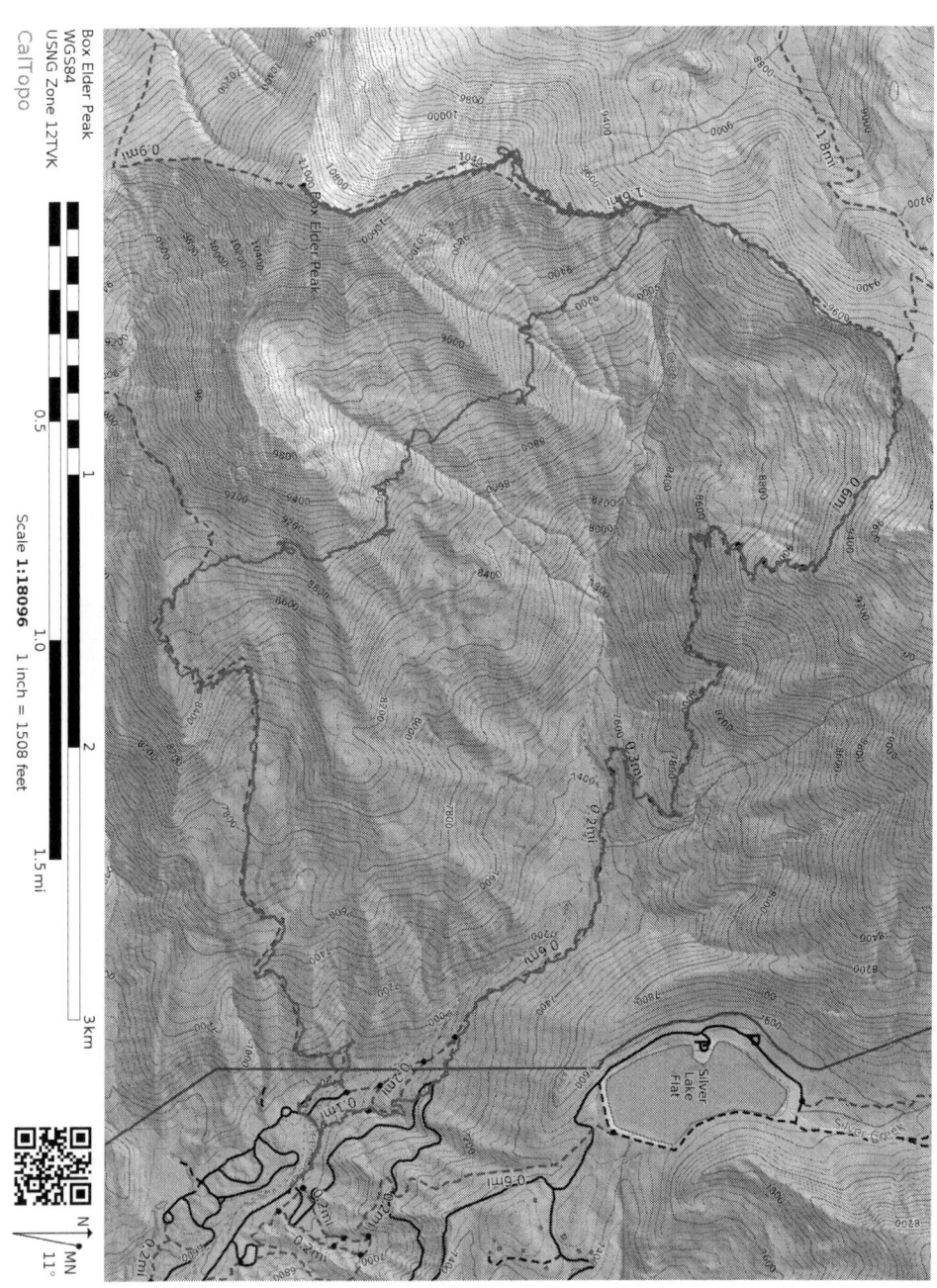

Hiking Gear
Checklist

YEAR ROUND

- Water (1-3 liters)
- Food
- Map or Gaia GPS app
- Sun protection
- Headlamp + batteries
- First Aid kit
- Hat
- Bandana or buff
- Insect repellent
- Trekking poles
- Grocery bag for trash
- Knife
- Camera
- Cell phone
- Kleenex
- Satellite Communicator like ZOLEO

WINTER

- Microspikes
- Extra Gloves
- Gaiters
- Extra Wool Socks
- Outer shell jacket
- Hand warmers
- Beanie
- Thermos of hot tea or hot chocolate

DOGS

- Water (1 L Minimum)
- Poop Bags
- Dog First Aid Kit
- Emergency dog booties

WWW.GIRLONAHIKE.COM

About the Author

Alicia Baker is the owner of "Girl on a Hike", a blog that follows Alicia and her hiking companion, Charlie, a Golden Lab, on their outdoor adventures. She has lived in Utah since 2013 and loves exploring everything from the High Uintas to the San Rafael Swell and desert. Each year, she and Charlie hike and backpack an average of 700 miles. "Girl on a Hike" has been awarded as one of the Top 100 Outdoor & Hiking Blogs from 2016 through 2020. She is also the author of "Salt Lake City's Best 52 Hikes", available only on Amazon. You can reach out to her on Instagram & Facebook @GirlonaHike.

Photo Credit: Halie West.

Find her on Instagram at @haliewestphoto

Made in the USA
Las Vegas, NV
29 March 2022

46504761R00085